IF THINGS DON'T IMPROVE SOON I MAY ASK YOU TO FIRE ME:

The Management Book For Everyone Who Works

If Things Don't Improve Soon I May Ask You to Fire Me:

The Management Book For Everyone Who Works

RICHARD K. IRISH

Anchor Press/Doubleday
Garden City, New York
1975

Library of Congress Cataloging in Publication Data

Irish, Richard K
If things don't improve soon I may ask you to fire me.

Includes index.
1. Personnel management. I. Title.
HF5549.I66   658.3
ISBN 0-385-08357-2
Library of Congress Catalog Card Number 74–12710

To All who labor in the vineyards of the Lord, whether you press the grapes or work in "Top Management": May your children grow fat in the New Jerusalem.

CONTENTS

ACKNOWLEDGMENTS

Writing a book is my idea of a grunt job.

All my life I lived happily without knowing what a gerund is. And who the hell cares about those dangling participles and split infinitives; conjunctions that should be semicolons and semicolons that want secret lives as ellipses? Well, writing a book means painstaking attention to these little gremlins.

My agent, Don Cutler at Sterling Lord; Warren Wiggins, my boss at TransCentury; and Loretta Barrett, my editor at Anchor Press, all gave me encouragement to write this book. Bill Josephson, Victor Hirsch, and General William Thompson (Ret.) made useful suggestions. John Evans and David Rice made special contributions. *The Resume Place* in Washington, D.C., also was helpful in providing me with original material for which I am grateful. My thanks to all of them.

Yeoman work was done by Penny Saffer, who typed the manuscript from my notes, which looked more like an FBI raw data file than a book's first draft. Patricia Aburdene brought real editorial flair to bear on the text. My sincere thanks to both of them. I wish to acknowledge, as well, an article in *Society,* January 26, 1973, written by Douglas Powell and P. F. Driscoll, which I adapted for Chapter Five in this book, entitled "Middleclass Professionals Face Unemployment."

Of course, I take full blame for any deficiencies in the book. I'll also welcome any rounds of applause.

A vote of thanks to everyone I've worked with on the job, including the thousands I've interviewed, all of whom were grist for my writing mill: Let this book be a tribute to our experience together and a modest gift of love.

Finally, a special thank you to my wife, Sally, who put up with my bad temper while I tried to figure out whether those damn gerunds wanted to be nouns or verbs.

R. K. IRISH

July 8, 1974
Marshall, Virginia

PROLOGUE

"If things don't improve soon, I may ask you to fire me!"

Which a few years ago, a person who worked for *me,* for heaven's sake, had the cheek to say.

It made me want to cash in my retirement benefits, forgo an outrageously high salary, throw away my stock options, hang up my jock, and follow Holy Orders. Fortunately, cool heads prevailed, and a strong desire to meet the monthly mortgage payment caused me to rethink my position and write a book, instead, about how to find a good job.

The result was *Go Hire Yourself an Employer,* a slim book on how to find a job; a lot of people liked it. It encouraged me to write what's here. Which is all about what happens when you do find a job. And the hard job of finding good people for tough jobs . . . and what to do when an employment relationship turns sour. Great bedside reading!

As such, this book is another "how to" book intended for everyone who wants help in the business of hiring, firing, and working with people. So, you conclude, the book is for managers—people who manage people.

Well, yes . . . and no.

The book is meant for a much larger audience:

• Those interested in organizational behavior should latch onto an idea or two.

• The unhappily employed (who need all the help they can get) in figuring out the mentality of the managerial classes.

• People who regularly hire and fire—that is, those anointed by Top Management, heaven forfend, to wield the executive scepter of the Appointing Power.

• Unemployed white-collar workers, down in their luck and into the soup.

• And it's for everyone who has punched a time clock, had to fire their best friend, or been exquisitely "selected out" by the Organization.

No, the book is not limited to managers—there have been more books written by him, for him, and about him than Napoleon Bonaparte. Rather, it is intended for both those who hire for important jobs as well as those hired: one no more writes a sensible book about the whole employment game from the manager's standpoint than one writes a book about, say, marriage from one partner's point of view.

The whole business of hiring/firing is an obvious fifty-fifty proposition, a reciprocal relationship, a racket game of service, volley, and returns.

An endless game. Where there are far more losers than winners. Winning, by the way, is defined as someone who is a happy, effective, and achieving personality on the job no matter whether he is in Top Management or works as a deckhand.

Another central theme of this book is: No matter what side of the desk you *think* you sit on, every day in every way, you are both someone's employer and someone's employee, this person's nominal superior, that person's, terrible expression, subordinate. A clear picture of what is happening between both parties (or even among third, fourth, and fifth parties in your giant organizations) is best observed from all points of view *at the same time*. To view it otherwise is to establish a false and mischievous dichotomy between those who boss and those who obey (rare, indeed, except in the Church and the 82nd Airborne Division), between the governors and the governed, between the shepherd and his sheep, as we shall see.

Throughout the book, when I speak of managers, I use the personal pronoun "he." But, of course, with more and more women in the management marketplace and many more who want jobs, there is clearly an urgent need on the part of men like me, who write about management, to focus on distaff management when appropriate. So, when I write "he" in the text, I mean "she," too. Effective leadership within organizations has no sexual bias (nor does ineffective leadership, for that matter). Men and women act much the same way on the job. But each sex *perceives* the opposite sex *on the job* in ways that require some elaboration. My observations on the whole subject are, of course, qualified by my being a man. Objectivity on the subject of the sexes is impossible —both on and off the job—because all of us are prisoners of our gender. But I do believe it is possible to be "objective" about how managers should hire and fire. And if this approach undermines the male management *macho* ("We must never fire a woman because she is dependent on *our* protection and besides it would hurt her feelings") or outrages female liberationists ("We are barred by a male conspiracy from access to power") then your disappointment in my observations is simply another reflection of these interesting times!

The book *is* limited in the *kind* of employment it analyzes. This book is *not* about employment situations and trends among the great masses of employed—that is properly a field best left to manpower analysts, nor is the book aimed at any special group—industry, government, the service sector, or the philanthropies. All organizations have a common disposition toward hiring and firing, whether it's IBM or the CIA. The book is certainly not about the "personnel process," which is anathema to growing people and organizations. Rather, the book is restricted to certain kinds of jobs—what Bob Townsend calls "judgment jobs" or what academics refer to as "knowledge jobs," occupations where you are paid for doing much more than filling a slot or being another cog in the industrial paperwork machine.

Judgment jobs are, in a word, where you are paid for the quality of the decisions you make, for your imagination in transcending organizational structure, for the energy and leadership you contribute on specific problems or tasks—jobs where the human personality makes *the* difference, jobs more important than any job titles or description satisfactorily comprehends; the kind of jobs all of us want; that are hard to find and that we often create for ourselves, and for which there are never sufficient candidates.

Another theme of the book is the importance of taking risks. (Pay attention, now—you will be quizzed on this later.) "High risks, high gain" is my boss's favorite expression—the risk-taking propensity everyone needs to cultivate, that is, the ability to welcome personal confrontations, to face up to "people problems." The effective Organization Man (or woman) is one who puts people first, addressing a person's strengths and matching those assets against an organization's objectives. "There are no 'wrong' people—simply people in wrong jobs." A shorthand summation of what I want to say is, "Nobody should be hired for his weaknesses." But, of course, it happens all the time.

I urge people, both employers and employees, to take risks, which is the reason most people avoid hard decisions—how to change an organization, which is to say, how to work with and turn over people (without driving everyone crazy), which means taking chances.

Who said, "Hell is other people?"

Probably one of those Russians. Well, on the job, hell is other people: your boss, who hasn't said "good morning" to you for a week; his boss, who doesn't know your first name; your three assistants, who say "good morning" (and nothing else the whole day); and the ten people who work for them, to whom you always forget to say "good morning."

I fancy I see the employment process wholly and clearly. I hired a few hundred key people for a hot-shot government agency back in those heady pre-Watergate days when we asked what we could do for our country, only to find out what it was doing to us! And then for five years I helped found and manage TransCentury Corporation, a private management services corporation. At the same time, I managed an executive search component for the organization, finding hard-to-find people for a, uh, modest fee. In other words, I was a headhunter and learned a lot about employers. Most of them are as confused about what they want as the typical job seeker.

And lately, for the past three years, I've been working for organizations that need help in the "People Department": minority hiring for business, outplacement for the newly fired; teaching a job clinic for university grads, planning "recruitment strategies," as we say in our brochure for client organizations; and, smart aleck I am, writing books about it all.

Thus I've been in the business of hiring, firing, counseling, and brokering people for important jobs. As such I'm the man at the beginning of the employment pipeline . . . *and the end.* This gives me a synoptic view, a chance to grandstand on the two most important days in your organizational life: the day you're hired and the day you "quit."

In the course of my work I've had to counsel, congratulate, console, and occasionally give up on people. But, as you can tell, I love my work. That's the main reason I'm writing this book.

IF THINGS DON'T IMPROVE SOON I MAY ASK YOU TO FIRE ME:

The Management Book For Everyone Who Works

CHAPTER 1

"If things don't improve soon, I may ask you to fire me!"

The first part of this book is all about what you would normally expect to come last.

All about the importance of firing people. Even your best friend.

Robert Anderson, the playwright, says about monogamy what everyone should know about the employment process, "After two weeks in any marriage, there is grounds for divorce."

Thus the employment contract, like the conjugal covenant, presupposes the possibility (and even desirability) of separation. When you hired out for the job *you* fill, that was the day the seed of discontent was planted that grows into the sharp thistle you and your boss must learn to grasp. In other words, the day you were hired is the first day there was a *possibility* of quitting or being fired.

Understanding that there is *no such thing as a permanent job* (or a permanent relationship, although many last a lifetime) is central. Obviously, your employer has the freedom to fire you any time (or should in healthy organizations), and you have the freedom to quit any time (or should if you have a healthy mental outlook).

To know you can be fired (or quit) at any time, far from being the personal tragedy most people assume, is the essential precondition in a healthy working environment. Establishing this fact at the onset of an employment relationship frees both parties to the transaction—employer and employee alike—from feelings of obligation, dependency, and guilt, which hang like the Sword of Damocles over most employment transactions.

"Why do I hate to fire people?"

We say it's the worst thing about our jobs.

This is a cop-out.

It's management's pleasure to start and stop employment relationships. Posing as the nice guy too cruel to drop the guillotine is to subject plenty of people to the garrote—a far worse punishment.

Of course, nobody *likes* firing people.

With the exception of corporate bully boys hopelessly becalmed in midadolescence, during ten years in the business I've found no one who savors giving the ax to anyone. But in the business of managing for effectiveness and of keeping people's goals consistent with new organizational directions, there is simply no way management can avoid the crucial crunch of firing important people at the right time. How it should be done is an art every manager needs to know. Without this ability many managers themselves are candidates for the ax.

The reason people hate to fire people is that it causes pain. It means they reject another human being. Feeling pain at firing people is appropriate. The cop-out is not following through and doing it.

The pain derives from the intense involvement every healthy working environment demands. We learn about one another—and care. Our wives play tennis together, your boys go to the same summer camp, you got hilariously drunk together on your last out-of-town assignment: You have become colleagues, pals, hunting companions out to snare the pelf for the benefit of your families, yourselves, and the organization.

And the situation is no different if you happen to be a woman and are charged with the hiring/firing authority. The only difference is the names you might be called; instead of being labeled a "bastard" for cashiering, say a man, fifteen years senior to you, the lady who wields the ax will be called a "bitch." But, as we shall see, it is far better to be called names by those you show the door than to suffer the consequences of being a "nice woman who can't make a decision."

And now it's your job to discharge, terminate, mandatorily retire, separate, select out—the euphemisms are legion—the very man or woman who was a boon companion. And because you delay, others, doing the work, complain that you put personal feelings ahead of your job.

"So we should want to fire ineffective people?"

Not to do so demoralizes effective people.

In school, we *should* fail students. Not doing so harms those who do excellent work. We further cripple a poor performer when we insist he is in the same league with the best. We wreck the morale of those who make the sacrifices all excellence entails, while a favored few, warm and safe and cozy back at camp with the squaw types, barter on the chief's indulgence.

Avoiding the pain, delaying the inevitable, refusing to recognize that someone you like very much doesn't fit your organization any more is similar to the marriage where both spouses can't face the prospect of divorce: apathetic, indifferent, and evasive behavior works to conceal soluble anomalies between the two parties. And if the situation is allowed to suppurate, if both parties to this sick arrangement continue to block out personal responsibilities to themselves and the organization that pays them, the chances of change, the opportunities for a new matrix to congeal are dim indeed. The loser you won't fire could be a winner elsewhere. For both of you, the risk-taking approach is the only exit to freedom.

Yes, firing and being fired are painful. Most people think they can pass through the employment process *unmarked*. Some managers believe they can avoid hard decisions. Like passing through school without being graded or an outdoor pack trip without discomfort, no one enters and leaves the world of work without giving and suffering pain. Those who succeed in avoiding the pain of firing (or being fired) stand charged with the crime of never having lived.

"That's a helluva sweeping organization. Can you back it up?"

Well, er, yes.

In tough, knowledge jobs where performance and results count, where people's contributions are easily perceived, where the bottom line is writ in the blood of the people who bleed for the organization, people are bound to disappoint one another. There is no way expectations can be entirely fulfilled after the honeymoon period wanes. Both parties to the employment relationship making beautiful music together is a fiction carefully cultivated by human relations, "touchy feely" administrators, all of whom dread conflict situations.

It's not in the stars, Horatio.

People are changing, like organizations, all the time. Business conditions, dynamic and unpredictable, make the People Problem highly idiosyncratic. Only steady attention to this *constant* state of change prepares managers for the tough decisions they singly can make. And anyone who hires, by definition must know how to fire—because this year's *Wunderkind* is next year's company scapegoat.

"What happens when people aren't fired on the job?"

An outside management consultant starts yammering about a "communications failure"; at least one of your people quits "on principle." The boss seems hard to talk to suddenly; neither of you feels free with the other; suddenly people have time to think about a lot of unimportant matters, such as their relative standing on the organizational chart; the imagined slur on the part of your secretary; why his recent raise was only one half, for Christ's sake, that of Charlie Brown, who's ten years *younger* than he is!

For the first time at Sticky Wicket, Inc., he starts writing and, what's worse, reading memos!

"But surely not everyone is a candidate to be fired . . . or shelved?"

How many people work for the Ford Motor Company?

Five hundred sixty-seven thousand?

How many people are president of the company?

That's right, one.

Absurd, ladies and gentlemen, that any one of us can reasonably expect to "reach the top." In other words, somewhere up the corporate ladder each of us hits his ceiling. Somebody is going to start signaling, "This high . . . and no higher."

That's why every colonel is a secret failure: He never made general.

Why every general is a closet also-ran: He never jumped to the Joint Chiefs.

That's why everyone, at some time or another, wakes up to discover that the American Dream is his own personal nightmare. "The bitch goddess of success" drinks the blood of another victim.

I see her prey every working day—the "in, up, and shelved" population.

What a dreary commentary on the American ethos that all of us end up failures. That's what happens when you worship false gods.

"So, everyone, according to you, is a candidate for the pink slip?"

Many times in our occupational lives. Although most of us don't know it. After nine months, there are invariable signs of time's passage. On the jobholder's part, the following blips are picked up on his radarscope:

1. "When does a deserving person like me get a raise?"
2. "Why does my most elementary work require this nitpicking supervision?"
3. "Does the boss know his purchasing director is a chump?"
4. "Why, with what I've learned here, I could easily double my income and responsibility elsewhere."
5. "Good God, do I want to work with Anaconda Consolidated the rest of my life?"
6. "I need to fire all those drones and hire my own staff."
7. "Thank God it's Friday."

All of which signals foul weather ahead. At this point—managers and "the managed" alike—switch off their earphones. Instead of talking out their problem, people begin talking to themselves. That's why you say it's *bedlam* where you work. Crazy.

"How can managers tell when someone wants to quit or be fired?"

Your secretary recently can't seem to finish important assignments.

A project director in Buffalo doesn't return your phone calls.

The project's budget analyst is taking three-hour lunches and caught flu four times last winter.

Your special assistant is turning out sloppy work and spends a good hour a week making Xerox copies of his résumé.

Boy, are you in trouble!

A lot of people who report to you are sending messages, the gist of which is, "Help, up there! If things don't improve soon, I may ask you to fire me!"

"Are you saying this is a confusing situation for both the boss and someone who works for him?"

It's bewildering.

On the one hand, the person who works for you is saying to

himself, "I wanta quit this job." On the other hand, he is sending a confused message to the executive suite, "Please fire me, I can't cope."

And you, the boss, are as confused as well. On the one hand, you're saying to yourself, "I oughta can this guy." On the other hand, you start sending signals like, "Please quit, I can't cope!"

"You mean, the boss sends out signals, too?"

Yes, indeed.

The message is sent in a thousand codes, but the meaning is the same: "Please quit and get off my back."

Here are some examples of how employers think:

"I'll temporarily detail Brown to work for Green—they hate each other's guts."

"Sure, I've sent Brown every year to our annual conference; let's send Blue this year."

"At our next staff meeting, I'll ask Brown's opinion—*last*."

"I'll tell Brown to fire Gray—they play golf together every Saturday."

"Sounds to me like an organizationwide communications problem."

No, indeed.

People are communicating like crazy. That's why it's like Bedlam where you work. Everyone is crazy as hell. As the boss, you are probably as confused as everyone else:

1. As the manager you've become bored, out of touch with your key people, and unimpressed with your own performance. Chances are good your boss should fire you—except the boss doesn't know it . . . *yet.*

2. The last time you had a heart-to-heart with your program people was a year ago when you passed out the company bonuses. They are not the same people *now,* and, it turns out, neither are you.

3. The objectives of your project are changing, and you don't like the direction that is telegraphed in bold type to your best people. How long is it since you've sat down with your boss?

4. Your people are growing restless; maybe they don't like the

project's current objectives. Or their own personal objectives are no longer consonant with the project's. The nine-month rule switches on: After nine months on any job, most people have mastered its essentials, met the key players, recognized that their job is not fulfilling new personal agendas. When you talk with them, they stare into the middle distance. "This guy doesn't throw off sparks any more," you think.

"Well, damnit, let them quit!"

You gotta be kidding!

No one is going to walk in your office, slam the door, pound on the desk, and shout, "I'm not taking any more, J.B., I quit!"

The last time that happened was in an old Kirk Douglas movie, circa 1952.

Besides, the kind of people sending you the Message are themselves so confused, so terrified of their own feelings that in the act of charging into your office they would certainly trip over the door stop!

No, ineffective and unhappy people on the job are no more able to confront you and quit than you can confront and fire them.

For your part, a similar evasive pattern emerges.

The new face in the office is gradually becoming part of the landscape—the new gunner hired to move and shake things up is a beached whale. Great expectations have been dashed.

"O.K., wise guy, have you ever been fired?"

No, and neither have you.

That's just the point. Nobody is fired in America any more. Because it hurts people's feelings. What happens is far worse. We are passed over for promotion, blocked from the next logical step in an organization, shelved. All the time management is telling us via the house organ how valuable Our People are as a natural resource. No, what's happened to me has happened to you . . . not the electric chair, but solitary confinement. Not a straight message in plain Anglo-Saxon, but a Chinese translation.

Not a healthy scolding; instead, the Dale Carnegie treatment.

And as for "human feelings," what is more unfeeling than to let someone "turn . . . and twist slowly in the wind?"

"Isn't the real reason we hate to fire people (and be fired) the social stigma attached?"

Yes.

Remember, at one time, a few hundred years ago, it was a sin to work at a job. "Oh, Henderson, yes, he's in *trade,* you know." Anyone who *needed* to work was a social outcast. This stigma gradually disappeared. With a little help from all of us, the stigmata of being fired can be made to disappear as well. Practically every capable person I know has admitted coming close to being fired. A lot of people anticipate a lousy job situation and quit. Still, most people lie low in a bad situation; instead of immediately starting a new job hunt, finding a job they want, and gracefully leaving a dreary situation, they wait and hide their real feelings from themselves and their employers and die the slow death of the occupationally dissatisfied.

"O.K., why can't I fire people and why won't they quit?"

Because neither party to this sickly transaction feels independent: you, the boss who needs a job done; nor your evasive, ineffective, Buffalo project director.

You counted on him to do a job; he counted on you for "support." Both of you characters are so dependently abject you truly deserve each other. Another employment marriage made in heaven.

Besides, the person who would quit (and who you should fire) *panics* at the thought of finding another job. Secretly, if someone quits, he worries, "I will never find another job"; secretly, you think, "If I fire him, no one will ever work for me again."

A standoff.

That's when you start sending messages! In Chinese. That's why we call where you work the Funny Farm.

"Chinese answers? Sounds like my boss's lingo!"

It's the language of "human relations" administration.

You get a Chinese answer when you have been cut out of the cable traffic, or your best secretary is transferred to another division, or you are no longer minuted on "eyes only" memos, or you are relegated to a mezzanine office, or your task force suffers a sharp budget cutback for no *apparent* reason.

All signs that Top Management is making, or has made up its mind about you . . . the fair-haired youth of yore. So, naturally, you ask for a meeting with your boss. And if it's some time coming, be sure Top Management wants you to quit and slink silently out the tradesman's entrance.

At last, grabbing the boss in the hall or over the water cooler, you discuss why you weren't consulted about a matter normally within your executive purview, like your secretary, the cable traffic, the budget cutback, or your new office with the five-foot ceiling.

His answer is usually an executive mumble, an on-the-one-hand, on-the-other-hand kind of reply that leaves you with the mystifying feeling that someone is trying to order Peking duck in a Shanghai restaurant—all in Gaelic. The point of the conversation is that your normally gruff, no-nonsense boss has an opinion about you that is painful for him in the extreme to share, particularly with you—the principal actor.

So, when you get the Chinese answer to the most important question you can ever ask, "Am I really making a contribution here?," know ye you've been sandbagged.

The doubletalk syndrome, the Chinese answer, the evasive messages management is sending you in Mandarin code are the tipoffs that you best seek employment elsewhere.

For many who don't know the code or can't face its meaning, this ambiguous execution is the worst trauma of their occupational lives.

Some never recover.

And grow cautious on the next job, fearing the Chinese executioner above all else.

"Well, O.K., most managers don't know how to let people go. How come so many people leave anyway?"

Of course, no one is ever "fired" as such. The face-saving mechanisms being much in favor.

Asiatic.

Whenever you read or hear of someone leaving an organization for "family reasons," you can be sure someone just got the ax. Or announcement of early retirement. Or statements like "regretfully leaving the firm for a job I simply could not turn down" (almost always undesignated)—these and plenty more examples are typical reflex actions of people performing an organization *pas de deux* and saving face.

But the most popular way organizations rid themselves of people is to induce them to resign or retire through use of the carrot rather than the stick. Organizations pay plenty to clean out the executive suite through schemes such as huge separation allowances, increased retirement bonuses, buying out executives' contracts, and even persuading other companies to hire them.

Moving the corporate headquarters is another stratagem: Artful administrators persuade people the organization no longer wants to stay put rather than uproot family and move with the company to another town. People get the message, but never admit its meaning. It preserves the ego.

The gist of high-level management's problem is guts. Someone up there doesn't want you but is too frightened to say so. The boss wants to find someone between you and him to do his bloody work. Both parties, even third parties, feel unbelievable stress because nobody *confronts* the problem, every player hoping the other will solve the situation, which patently is impossible without personal confrontations.

Thus, low-level organizational managers, the gray-collar echelons, are disposed of without too much damage to most managers' psyche because someone else is ordered to lower the boom. The manager is the lord high judge, but he designates an underling to be the executioner. Some organizations employ a *de facto* hatchet man, the general counsel or the boss's special assistant. Their real job is firing people the boss doesn't want to say "good morning" to any more. Thus, those who give the command are shielded from the ugly sight of the firing squad performing its dirty duty.

"What if there is no hatchet man?"

This is usually the case; the "system" fires you.

The worst indignity is to be fired by your company rival, the man or woman who inherits your part of the kingdom. Management with its baffling—nay, downright sneaky—ways designates your heir apparent to bring you the bad news. Galling. Brutal. Pre-Paleolithic. And it happens a hundred times a day throughout American industry.

Another device is to sanction medical discharge—corporate medical departments are manipulated to develop a physical rationale for an employee's early retirement. The hypocritic oath in action.

"You mean there's always someone else to do the dirty work?"

Not so much any more.

More and more frequently, firing someone cannot be delegated. A real colleague must be discharged, someone on a first-name basis, a fellow commuter in the business of belting the commonweal. And that's why firing has become such a painful subject in the executive suite, dominated, as it is, by increased democratization in manner and permeated with a false humanist ethic. Corporate benignity run amok.

"What about firing people en masse?"

The word comes down (it doesn't come down often enough) for you to cut back 25 per cent on your staff.

Most managers simply stop hiring and let attrition work its solution. Not too smart. Top Management has given the go ahead to eliminate a lot of dead wood (and nonjobs) in your domain. Why not make a deal: fire 50 per cent of your staff with the authority to take half the savings to apply to salaries of new people?

"What do you mean the word doesn't come down often enough?"

Top Management everywhere doesn't give the green light often enough to clean out the executive suite. In boom times, overhead costs for salaries and fringe benefits saddle organizations with responsibilities horrendously difficult to discharge in down times when the bears come out to play. The motto in growth organizations is a people policy which says, "Let's keep this place lean and mean." And that means heavy turnover in people. A salubrious side effect is an abundance of judgment jobs both in good times and bad. All of which would make it a lot easier on people who are fired or quit organizations; the "panic" of unemployment would become far more manageable, an opportunity for personal and professional growth rather than an excuse for despair.

"So it's really my duty, as a manager, to fire ineffective people?"

Doing one's duty is unnatural. It causes resentment, self-hate, and heartburn.

No, damnit, you should *want* to fire the incompetent.

Do you abhor your whole staff talking about your great administrative ability? Do you loathe it when you do your job well? Do you hate yourself when you yourself are competent?

Managers who know when, how, and who to fire are not ogres. They are helping themselves. Discharging the ineffective, turning over your staff to make things work, for a change, in your shop, is a compliment to your own competence and effectiveness. That's why you should *want* to do it. Managers who delay joining the issue, hate facing a major People Problem, buck the problem to another level, or start talking Chinese to the hired hands, self-destruct in their own (and other people's) eyes—a signal to Top Management that you yourself are now a candidate for the pink slip.

"What do managers say to you about firing people?"

"I like everything about my job except firing people."

That's what I hear from a lot of self-serving executive ineffectives, all of whom, by implication, are telling me what a fine fellow, deep down, they really are. . . .

I think they themselves are all candidates for early retirement.

"O.K. How does firing people help organizations?"

Herewith the Gospel:

1. That the most important constituents in an organization are those who manage it. Customers, suppliers, clients, workers, shareholders, and consumers are the target population in the annual report; but in the real world they are in second, third, and sometimes last place.

2. That organizational overhead—commercial, philanthropic, governmental, academic—is ten feet deep in pork: executive featherbedding, everywhere a product of corporate benignity, is rapidly reaching crisis proportions among the management classes.

3. That shaving direct costs, that is, overhead, which means firing people, is a valid and time-tested tool of Top Management.

4. That the Age of Affluence is ending and the Age of Malthus has begun. Supply-demand curves are beginning to cross on a whole series of raw materials. This economy of multiplying scarcity positively argues for greater management effectiveness, more productive and less expensive use of executive manpower, with a view to better products and services at a lesser cost.

5. That the enormous size of most institutions today, while regrettable, is largely inevitable, and that the exponential growth in executive employment at every level must be accompanied by a corresponding increase in productivity.

6. That finding effective people is still management's toughest responsibility.

7. That stress on "motivational" theory is horse puckey. The real issue is hiring effective and firing ineffective people. That all institutions, accordingly, need to reform their hiring and firing practices, which, as we shall see, obviates the problem of executive motivation. That failing reform, organizations face a disappointing future and perhaps no future at all.

If you disagree radically with any of the foregoing assumptions, "fasten your seat belt," as Bette Davis once said in the movies, "and get ready for a rocky ride."

"So 'Top Management' has a lot to learn about how to fire people?"

Yes!

Increasingly in our society, authority is no longer exercised vertically; hierarchical leadership is yielding to collegial association. That's one reason people are never fired, as such, any more.

"But aren't conditions created to discourage quitting?"

Yes, to be sure.

Paternalism.

Socialism for the middle classes, capitalism for the poor.

"Do your job and we will take care of you. Forever."

Found nearly everywhere these days, IBM, the Army Map Service, the Ford Foundation, the Smithsonian Institution.

More on this later. The point is that corporate benignity is strangling people and organizations.

When time comes to fire a key man in the executive suite, the tools to do the job right are not available.

"Kindness" kills.

Letters of resignation, for example, are typically arch, phony, and consistent with the best business practices of the Gilded Age. No, the real damage is done in private bloodletting.

Don't expect organizations to change overnight. Fifty years of "human relations" administration is not going to disappear in the twinkling of an eye.

But all of us who try to find self-expression within organizations can do a lot about the Byzantine atmosphere where we work. But most of us won't. After all, we have our reputation as a Nice Person to protect.

"Is there any way to avoid this kind of unhealthy relationship on the job?"

Managers should conduct themselves with an on-the-job personality and an off-the-job approach to avoid this dependent bind.

There should be clear indications from the beginning in any employment relationship that managers are by definition *dual* personalities. On the job, organizational objectives are a first priority; off the job, the effective manager wins respect from those who need to know they cannot trade on his friendship (which no one in his right mind wants to do with his boss).

Women managers must especially guard themselves from male subalterns who could fall into the habit of treating the boss lady like Mom or big sister—an easy emotional touch who men think might shy from direct confrontation with the hired hands. Men, too, need to keep their eye on the ball. If you work for a woman (I've worked for *four* women in my occupational lifetime and know whereof I speak), chances are, if you are of the old school, that you will try to *protect* the boss lady from bad news or pick up the marbles when she makes a mistake. That's your first mistake. The worst kind of patronization (and in this case, sexism) is for men to spare their employers—whether men or women—the painful and important job of hiring and firing. And both men and women whether "superiors or subordinates" need to remember that the only *difference* between them in living together within organizations is that some people are more accountable, managers, than others, employees.

Because there *must* be a difference; because there is a difference. The fraternity house atmosphere in the executive suite does more to wreck productivity, good employment selection processes, and organizational health than any other single influence. Even in the olden days, when the boss was a cranky, rugged individualist with sideburns, a Scrooge gone wild with the personnel ax, he was a damn sight better than the deliberate ambiguity and democratic centralism fostered by the false humanism and human relations orientation ever-present in many contemporary organizations. Managers—no matter at what level—need to cultivate the qualities of organizational detachment ("How can I do my job better today?") and intense interpersonal involvement ("How can Jim improve on the job today?") to show themselves capable of rising above the peer pressure that groups of people will always bring to bear on the insecure and weak-willed manager.

No one wants to hold the boss hostage.

"What do you mean, 'hold the boss hostage'?"

Power runs down and *up* in organizations. Plenty of ineffective people play on the weakness of management. They hold a gun to the boss's head and say, "You can't fire me."

"I'll slap a class action suit against this outfit."

"I've forgotten more about programming than you'll ever learn; fire me and the contract goes fizzle."

"I'll quit and take our secrets to the competition."

"Because if you do, this outfit's name is mud in Washington."

And on, and on, and on.

These are the real corporate terrorists who shamelessly traffic in kidnaped information, friendships, knowledge, and contacts to prevent managers from showing them the door. Blackmail.

Dependent on their jobs, they use veiled threats to make an organization dependent on them. Those who are the weakest appeal to the feelings of guilt they have cunningly inspired in their betters. Thus, some minority-group members can make an easy touch on a "liberal" manager. Other examples are:

• a technician who monopolizes a skill and becomes "indispensable" to management.

• those trafficking in trade secrets who sense how valuable they are to the competition.

• those disgruntled and helpless stink ants in organizations who cry "Foul" whenever they smell competence being rewarded.

• faculty with tenure, tenacious in their academic freedom, and bitter foes of the administration who don't have the freedom to fire them.

• the "very humble and weak" who say, "Look what a mess I am, don't fire me."

The list is obviously endless. The psychological warfare waged in organizations is by no means the exclusive province of management; its practitioners are found in jungle garb among the hired hands, and the ransom demanded is the security of their jobs.

"Yes, but you're not saying, I hope, that firing this person and hiring that one is the answer to all our problems?"

Hardly. After forty years on the planet I don't think there are totally satisfying answers to anything!

Now, of course, while it's true that there is no such thing as a permanent job; that job turnover in the best jobs in our society is legendary; that, accordingly, good men and women are constantly changing jobs to mesh against the changing conditions of our work environment; and even though it follows that smart managers need to fire people in order to free-up slots for able people, it does *not* follow that every manager—once he finally faces up to a confrontational situation—must necessarily *fire* the man or woman currently holding down the job.

Time and time again in my job, which is acting both as participant and observer to these inevitable and healthy People Problems, the very *act* of confrontation itself *solves* the problem. A new work environment, a new relationship, in fact, two new people emerge. Sensational. Practically occult.

What happens is that one party to a bad relationship—either an unhappy and increasingly counterproductive jobholder or his noncommunicating and withdrawing boss—takes the bull by the horns and sets the stage for a showdown. Both parties can now confront a *real* problem—namely, whether it's really worthwhile to continue such a half-assed relationship.

The result often is separation, divorce, final estrangement. Depending on who initiated the showdown, either the jobholder "quits" or his employer "asks for his resignation."

Which really doesn't make much difference.

More often than most people think, the result is salubrious from both parties' point of view: A new relationship begins to flame from the ashes.

If termination is not the result, the employer, in plain fact, has hired himelf a new employee. And the jobholder has himself a new boss.

By reasoning together, establishing new work objectives, ventilating personal concerns, and honestly exchanging criticism of each other, both parties re-establish the reasons they made this employment marriage in the first place. And maybe identify some additional compelling reasons, too.

"So it's really a People Problem when two parties to a disappointing situation don't want to face the fact there is a problem?"

What I'm saying is that the effective manager, the man or woman who wants to feel increasing self-esteem, a reward for personal growth on the job, needs to encourage, yes, *program* confrontations with the key people for whom he is responsible.

And, conversely, the smart jobholder initiates, if his own manager is laggard, these very same confrontations.

In other words, both parties need periodic personal confrontations with each other in order that both continue to grow as human beings. Most important, the organizational imperative needs to be served; the constant law of change within all institutions presumes that both parties are changing.

People within organizations fail at confrontation, fail as managers because they fail as people: They miss the central involvement of human interaction. This failure, what "experts" call a "communications breakdown" (which it is not), is encouraged in today's huge organizational matrixes. It is, in fact, the most obvious symptom of the "scale" problem, the problem of bigness.

Nobody in large organizations confronts other human beings.

Every administrative nostrum known to management science is used as a substitute—mandatory grievance committees, suggestion programs, human relations training, executive development programs;

all is Mickey Mouse makework to substitute *processes* as a replacement for individual confrontation.

Involvement.

That is the answer to People Problems.

And we hate involvement, preferring the manufactured processes of the manpower development experts, because we are afraid of the pain that is implied in all personal growth. And it *is* painful to confront a dilatory employee (or, conversely, an apathetic boss). But no matter what the outcome, whether both parties separate—that is, one party cleans out his desk and leaves the organization—or a *new* relationship develops, both people, the boss and the bossed, feel that realism has been served, that both, for a change, were adults. And both are bigger and more effective people for it.

"Involvement? I don't understand."

Firing someone, goddamnit, like hiring him in the first place, is being *involved*. If a committee, a process, or pre-employment testing programs are used by your organization to hire people, then small wonder that elaborate processes are used to fire people. What's missing is any *involvement* between two human beings.

"O.K. The trouble is that my people are afraid of me. It's damn difficult to become involved with them."

They defer to you, try to *please* you, feel *subordinate, dependent*.

A bad situation.

And it's as much their fault as yours. Involvement is a two-way street. Shrewd jobholders make it their business to understand your problems. The vast majority prefer the anonymity of the herd.

"What can I do to improve my skill in firing people?"

Tell the truth.

If someone is ineffective on your staff, he needs to know it. The first thing tomorrow morning, call him in and discuss it.

Second, is there someone on your staff you don't *like?* Why don't you like him? The day after tomorrow call him in and tell him so.

There are, therefore, two reasons people are fired: (1) they are ineffective; (2) the boss doesn't *like* them.

There are two reasons people "quit" jobs: (1) they feel ineffective; (2) they don't like the boss.

Tomorrow's meeting might be the first day of your business life you start feeling 100 per cent effective as a manager. Curiously, the exchange that will take place, far from being the most painful act of management, is the most liberating of experiences.

"Why?"

Both parties suddenly feel *free*.

Telling someone you don't *like* him or telling him why he is *ineffective, frees* both of you from third-party communication, the Chinese dialogue, the diplomacy of nondirect discourse.

The resulting improvement in your relationship is phenomenal. Even if you fire him or he quits.

"Are you saying that management doesn't tell people the truth?"

That's right.

The single greatest mistake management makes is not to tell the truth. How is a person to learn from an experience, how can we learn from our mistakes if management won't level?

"But you admit that firing, and being fired, are painful?"

But *not* firing ineffective people is what causes you and them the most pain.

They feel the pain because they sense something's wrong but don't know what.

And as for you, the dull pain somewhere between your endocrine gland and bile duct disappears, like any other onerous job accomplished, once the matter of firing someone is faced.

That's the pleasure, too. Doing your job well means firing people to make room for other people better able to fulfill organizational objectives. Why should that be painful to either party? Who wants to pursue a bad relationship? That's why the newly fired always feels unaccountable elation when the ax has fallen.

No, the real reason—this is from the bottom of my heart—you hesitate to fire people is that you secretly loathe the feeling of competence, potency, and effectiveness many people feel when they do a job right. And you at thirty thousand dollars per annum!

As for the jobholder, if he quits—puts an end to this on-the-job charade—he too feels enormous growth in self-esteem.

So, while you won't receive any singing telegrams from the people you fire, if you do the job right, I'll bet the cashiered party will have an increased respect for your competency and will hold far less ill feeling than you would suppose.

"What about quitting—how do I do it?"

The same way.

Ask for an appointment first thing tomorrow morning. Tell the boss why you feel ineffective on the job or why you don't *like* him. Suddenly you feel *free!* At last both of you are acting like adults.

Don't do unto others as they have done to you.

Every time you need to tell the boss something important, for your sake and his, don't start semaphoring in Chinese. And when you need to confront your people, don't practice the guileful tactics of a process server.

The best way to think through the People Problem is to look deeply into yourself and ask how you, in similar circumstances, would want to be treated.

Most people, unhappily, practice on others what has happened to them: We repeat the mistakes of our fathers. Break the cycle, now! Far from hating yourself in the morning, you'll be surprised at how good you feel.

"That sounds great. But suppose my boss fires me?"

You didn't resign; he didn't "fire" you. The relationship simply terminates. And what is so bad about terminating a bad relationship?

The firing process, like the hiring procedure, is a fifty-fifty proposition, a reciprocity between two human beings. I have a job for which I pay you money; you have the time and the talent to do the job. Ergo, you are "hired." In like manner, I find your work unacceptable or I can't function with you on the job (that is, "I don't like you"); you find my leadership unacceptable and can't function with me on the job (that is, "you don't like me").

In the first instance—the hiring process—I hired an employee; you hired an employer. In the second example—the firing process—I fired an employee; you "quit" a job.

The truth is simple . . . and liberating. No one is ever fired or quits. All that happens is that a relationship terminates. In a divorce action, who divorces who? On the job, the same thing.

"I still can't bear the idea of firing someone. Why?"

It "hurts" peoples' feelings.

But *not* firing people who are (1) ineffective or (2) not likable, is authentically hurting your feelings. In like manner, doing bad work or secretly disliking the boss (which you communicate in a thousand nondirect ways) is hurting yourself far more.

"But, my God, telling someone I don't like them—I've never done that before in my life!"

That's a confession of executive ineffectiveness and personal impotence. "I never met a man I didn't like." You and Will Rogers. Both of you are among America's foremost humorists. There is no way we can proceed from birth to death on this planet *liking* everyone. A *non sequitur*. A crime against nature.

Telling someone you don't like *him* frees that person to tell you why he doesn't like *you*. Incredibly, after this exchange, both of you are going to *like* each other a lot better. That's why we don't necessarily *fire* people or quit an employer we don't like.

"Why do we dislike each other less after this kind of exchange?"

Both of you feel "free." And feeling free and *acting* freely, for a change, is better than two double martinis, on the rocks, with a twist of lemon.

That's why people who are fired ("quit") or who do the firing feel so strangely elated once the task is done. But it's not so strange, because human elation is caused by acting freely. Both of you are going to feel *so good* about yourselves, the chances are better than even that this employment relationship won't terminate at all! Start acting *freely* with all your staff, and in a few months people will say, "Now, Charlie Brown, that fellow's *some* manager!"

"Is it easy to learn how to act freely with people?"

For most of us, including your humble correspondent, it's the hardest thing in the world. The most effective managers I've observed, however, are those who simply are "freer" on the job than their counterparts. Acting freely means:

1. Putting your own feelings first.
2. Sharing those feelings with those who "cause" them, including the boss.
3. Welcoming other people, including the boss or your least effective worker, to share their feelings with you.

All of which means you might find out some rather disturbing and painful information about your leadership style.

"O.K. But how do I act 'freely' with my boss who wants me to fire someone who is the most effective person in my shop?"

I think the "free" response to an example like this is quietly to inform the boss that you make the hiring/firing decisions in your department. At the same time, the boss has every right to *comment* and even evaluate your people's work. But only *you,* the accountable and responsible party, can make the decision. In this instance, you want *facts:* why does your boss want to cashier someone you regard as vital to your project? Maybe the reasons are sound and you should! But chances are good that your boss doesn't have all the information. So when he says, "Fire Harriet," that's your signal to marshal a good case why Harriet shouldn't be sacked. Moreover, to complicate matters further, maybe Harriet isn't the problem; maybe your relationship with the boss is what this crazy mixup is all about. All the more reason for a "free" exchange with the boss. Let's hope you have a lot more like it.

"Acting freely on the job seems too risky to me!"

The bold approach—both with those you work for and with those who work for you—means feeling free to vent personal feeling. The highest compliment which can be paid you, as a manager, is from time to time for the key people in your shop to "blow sky high" in your presence. That's why everyone wants to work for you!

"Won't frequent confrontations cause anxiety among my staff?"

What's wrong with that?

A little anxiety keeps people awake and thinking and alive!

Conflict is necessary before there are solutions; there must be a complete airing of the room. And this is the *point* of confrontations—to put problems out on the table so both parties can see them. Which, as any manager admits, is the major problem in most organizations, what masquerades as "a communications problem." But now it's out front, no longer a "communications problem"—a management problem. What you're paid a great deal of money to solve.

"Firing someone this way means he won't take it personally?"

Nay! A thousand nays!

That's the whole point. Firing someone, like hiring him in the first place, is a *personal* matter. The whole process of winnowing the chaff from the wheat means rejecting another human being, saying no, risking unpopularity. Which is what you should want to do if you don't want a visit from the Chinese executioner yourself.

Firing someone is damn personal. If the pink slip is handed out, or the "Chinese Spoken Here" signs appear, or a cushy nonjob for Harry Hasbeen is created, then nothing, least of all realism or honesty, has been served.

"I'm glad you *did* take it personally" is what a boss should say to someone shown the door. How can anyone grow, that is, learn from his mistakes, unless he learns *personally?*

And, in like manner, how can "management" learn about itself if people who "quit" don't level with the brass?

"What do you do when appointed to a new job and half your staff are incompetents?"

Wait a week. Identify the worst performer in the group.

Call him into your office and fire him. In one day's time every person on your staff will show dramatic improvement.

"That's great, but didn't you already say, as managers, we should want to fire people who are ineffective?"

That's right. I'm glad the lessons are taking hold!

In the case of a *new* boss, however, in point of plain fact, you, the chief, must *rehire* the whole staff you inherit. And if you are one of the worker bees, be sure that if a new man or woman is brought in from the outside your first job is to reckon whether you want to hire this new employer.

No doubt about it. One reason Top Management fires the top dog and brings in new blood is to shake your department up. And invariably this means lots of people start looking for jobs elsewhere. There's nothing like a new hired gun in the catbird's seat to rouse the benchwarmer from his natural bureaucratic torpor.

So as the new gunner in town, *be sure* your newly acquired staff *expects* a dust-up. In my years, I've watched at least thirty hired guns brought in to shake up the place. In some cases, I've concluded that the new organizational directions implied in the change of command were not my cup of tea; in other cases, I've secretly cheered the new man or woman on and psychologically re-established myself with the organization. In none of these thirty instances can I remember being indifferent.

The best time, therefore, for you, as the newly appointed accountable authority, dramatically to change the tone, direction, and substance of your department is very soon after coming on the job. People *expect* you to make changes. Don't disappoint them.

"Swell. But suppose I inherit a crackerjack staff?"

You should be so lucky!

So nobody is shown the door. But that doesn't mean you don't have a long heart-to-heart talk with every man and woman on board. All of which is preliminary to your making individual decisions about each person, all of which ratifies your leadership position while at the same time providing you with the information you need to change staff assignments.

"How would you fire an incompetent?"

Find out what his incompetency is costing your firm.

Start with his salary. If he is paid eighteen thousand dollars per year and isn't performing, he is losing your firm money.

If he makes frequent mistakes, cost out the expense of these snafus. The time, for example, it takes to correct his errors is easily measurable in dollars.

Figure out the total cost to your organization for keeping him on the company dole.

There is an organic relationship between work and pay. Highlight this connection when you fire someone. "Buster, you cost this firm $3,256 last month. Let me show you how."

If your facts are right, this technique works every time.

"Is that a good technique to use on people you are not going to fire?"

Every payday. One by one you call your people in for a five-minute chat before you hand out the pay envelopes. This routine has a remarkable effect on people; it reminds them of the casual relationship between work and survival.

For reasons best understood by clinical psychologists, people deliberately forget they are paid for what they *do*. A salary check comes to be expected every fortnight. The old-fashioned custom of the boss handing out the greenbacks is largely a thing of the past. Make it part of your leadership routine. The effect will be astonishing.

"So you don't think being fired or doing the firing is the worst part of going to work each day?"

Not if people stop being afraid of each other.

My thesis is simple.

Being fired or doing the firing is vital to organizations. There is a right way to do it.

And if it's done right, it's ten to one that both parties salvage what was best in their relationship.

An employment relationship, after all, is a business relationship —not a fraternal bond. There is no way it can be. And business relationships are among the most satisfying established in a lifetime. But such relationships need constant renewal and renovation. Who's to say a severed relationship can't be re-established in another environment on different terms at a later date?

"Are you saying we only function well in jobs we feel free to quit?"

That's right.

And if we manage people, we only feel effective when we are free to "fire" them.

The key element, of course, is personal freedom. The person who feels dependent on his employer (and most people do) is never as effective as the individual who can turn his back on his employer, drop the gate, and find another job. That's why knowing how to job jump is so important; it gives a person the confidence to put his job on the line time and time again.

"Well, I'm still not convinced, but I'll read on. Any other advice?"

Keep two things in mind:

No manager should hire anyone for a "permanent" job. And no one is allowed to become indispensable in an organization.

Thus endeth the first lesson.

CHAPTER 2

The people problem

"What do you mean, there's no such thing as a permanent job?"

No one should perceive a job as a permanent *right*. Sound company policy is to establish this pre-eminent condition at the outset of an employment relationship, constantly underscored through personal confrontation. And if it comes to pass that both parties need to separate (the chances are good that both *want* it and are relieved that the other party feels the same way), then who is to say that industrial environments can't be made civilized work places, where people are reciprocal, open, and adult in their intercourse? The other course, the phony road of corporate benignity through the use of nondirect discourse, favored by impotents and ineffectives, is an invitation to corporate decline.

Spiritual bankruptcy.

Jobs must be big enough for people's spirit. The pity of our times is that most jobs demean and lessen the human personality. Organizations should have a self-interest in developing their people even if it means firing them. And if what animates institutions is a spirit of fair play and mutual reciprocity, then the confrontational process can come to be the transaction where people grow in experience, knowledge, and, finally, wisdom rather than the central trauma in most people's occupational lives.

"Why do so many people believe jobs are permanent?"

The cause of the curse is that people think jobs are "property." A piece of real estate to be bought and sold on an exchange. "This job *belongs* to me because I fill it; until I leave it, it is mine alone."

Of course, the "property" analogy is not a bad one; talent, skill, achievements, experience, and education, the accumulation of a lifetime are a person's "qualifications" or property. One does not "lose" one's talent when one loses a job. Rather, one's property is what we carry from one job to another, what a job candidate for a judgment job carries in his head. This can never be taken away from him.

But jobs are eliminated and created every day depending on the changing objectives of an organization, the business climate, and other events that nobody can *control*. So if your job is eliminated or if you must eliminate jobs and create others, the chances are good that events and outside forces govern your decision.

To "own" a job, the same way one would own, say, an expensive set of golf clubs, is irrational. But it happens all the time. Organizations that permit key people to think they are indispensable do a grave disservice to the people concerned (who are allowed to think a job is theirs for life), and cause organizations to lose sight of their real objectives—*which is* not *to take care of Freddie!*

"Don't take care of Freddie? But I thought a manager's responsibility was to his people?"

No, a manager's responsibility is for the *objectives* of the organization. His job is not to make Freddie happier, wealthier, or more comfortable. Only Freddie can do *that* by becoming progressively more competent, productive, and involved on the job. The organization isn't taking care of Freddie; Freddie's taking care of himself. And that's why he likes working where he does; he doesn't feel *dependent* on the organization because he is making a measurable, visible, and rewarded contribution to fulfilling the organization's objectives.

The happiest people in an organization are those moving in, up, and out. Some organizations encourage the five-year flush principle: everyone from the Chairman of the Board to the stenos in the executive secretariat must either significantly jump in terms of salary, responsibility, and productivity within five years or automatically exit from the organization. Not a bad idea. Particularly when it comes to hiring (and firing) the chief executive officer. My hunch is that five years is plenty of time to make his or her contribution. After that time, top managers tend to jade.

"So when people lose sight of organizational objectives, start printing up the pink slips?"

Which means most of us next Monday have a date at the employment security office. Not too likely.

Besides, anyone who uses a pink slip to fire the help (newspaper publishers, upon going out of business, favor this method) should be made to wear a dunce cap, sit on a tall stool in the corner, and read every annual report of their firm since Nineteen Naught Nine.

The terse mimeographed message is still far too common in institutions so large they are bigger than the people who work for them: A 30-year veteran of a major communications firm, who was making $45,000 per annum, saw his department and job wiped out with 350 strokes of a typewriter against letterhead bond; a three-time-wounded infantry officer, passed over for promotion the second time, saw his name in alphabetical order on a list of officers soon to leave the service; a manufacturer's representative with sales averages of $500,000 each year found his pink slip in the pigeonhole marked "Important Messages."

No wonder, according to recent polls, Americans now distrust institutions more than at any time since the beginning of public opinion research. This is mostly due to the politics of change in the last decade in America. But plenty of distrust stems from the way organizations *talk* to their people—the public relations blitz, the phony corporate compassion that inspires immediate distrust.

The only thing to be said for the pink slip is that it's slightly better than the Chinese message. At least it's a swift demise, not death by asphyxiation.

No, these men did not lose sight of organizational objectives, but the factors of their working environment were such that each reached his level of competence. There was a ceiling on each individual's "career." Or, simply, objective conditions changed and wiped out their jobs.

The communication company's vice president wasn't going into Top Management; the Army captain wasn't going to be invited to the War College; the manufacturer's rep would never manage the coveted Chicago territory.

Shelfsitters.

Productive shelfsitters.

"Well, what do you do about them?"

First of all (and more on this later), you tell them what the score is:

> Sticky Wicket, Inc. 10
> Harry Hasbeen 3

The first kind of shelfsitter sits on his hands—he isn't effective, isn't "growing," isn't doing his job.

The second kind of shelfsitter is effective, isn't "growing" either, but *is* doing the job.

The first needs to be shown the door, *pronto;* the second needs a warm slap on the back and some straight talk from Top Management. To wit, there's no place to go at Sticky Wicket.

"Didn't you say everybody someday hits his ceiling?"

That's right.

The plain facts are that everyone *someday* is Harry Hasbeen. Unless we violate the Peter Principle and are not promoted to our level of incompetence. For plenty of people, the day we know we won't replace Robert McNamara at the World Bank is the first time we realize the inevitability of our occupational mortality, recognize our limitations.

For others, who love their walk of life, that is, they like selling, soldiering, and managing, rising to the ceiling of their institutional environment is not like walking the plank. "In, up, and out" is half true—it keeps up the body tone of the institution. But there is a place for performing executives able to change with changing organizational objectives, so long as Top Management is frank about their promotional prospects. That way neither party has unrealistic expectations of the other.

Productive shelfsitters need to be told, however, that (1) younger and abler people are not to be denied; (2) that their jobs, in any event, are not permanent; (3) that their performance will continue to be judged on the basis of productivity, and (4) that no middle-management sabotage will be tolerated.

"Is that the risk taker's approach to managing the shelfsitter?"

The bold approach. But boldness is the way you solve People Problems. The chances are good that the bold approach will cause an enormous increase in morale. The truth has a way of setting people free.

"Great, but how do you motivate the shelfsitter?"

Haven't I heard this tune before? Nobody, friends and readers, can motivate anyone else.

Nobody, for example, can "motivate" me to make a million dollars.

I can motivate me; you can motivate you.

The same with shelfsitters.

Bribe him with more money? Harry Hasbeen likes it—we all do. Don't tell him he doesn't deserve it; that wouldn't be "nice." But more swag won't make Harry hustle.

Try education. Retool Harry for a new job. Expensive and chancy. The chances are good that Harry will use this company-financed downtime to rethink his future, and Sticky Wicket won't be in it. Which is a costly strategy if that's what you want Harry to do— leave the firm. Far better to show him the door.

Job enrichment? Sounds great and is the new industrial panacea we read about so much lately. The problem is that it won't work. Old attitudes come home to roost despite Harry's new job (which he didn't want so much as you wanted it for him); his new working conditions are rapidly the routine scenery for his continued lack-luster productivity. Doesn't it make more sense to fire Harry and find someone who has the motivation?

Tell Harry what the score is. No more boosts in pay, better jobs, new working conditions, educational credits, and other goodies from the treasurer's cash box without demonstrated, visible, increased productivity.

"Everything you say makes sense and is terribly macho, but I can't bring myself to hatchet a loyal employee after years of service."

Nobody says you must chop his head off—yet.

Some shelfsitters are vital to organizational stability—so long as they do the job and don't zap the young and spirited. And the reason is that their real objectives in life aren't found on the job in your organization.

Shelfsitters:

- moonlight at their real vocation while they collect a paycheck at your firm.
- pursue some obsession (like sailboating, Boy Scouting, back-gammon), which your firm finances.
- lead secret lives, write novels, jog, culture vulture—all of which are made possible by the dumb job they hold at your firm.

Chalk up Harry as a loyal company man. Tell him what the score is. Make him tell you what his hidden agendas are. Two parties taking each other into mutual confidence resolves whether to show Harry the door or keep him in his fur-lined rut at Sticky Wicket, Inc.

"Well, you say, change is necessary, but where I've worked, all the orders flow from above."

Organizations like:

- ITT
- the U. S. Navy
- the Roman Catholic Church
- the U. S. Department of Health, Education and Welfare
- Pan American World Airways

Not exactly your Mom and Pop organizations, nor exactly people-centered, and from all accounts in deep trouble. All the above institutions and a thousand more like them suffer from (1) an overhead overload, (2) giantism, (3) vertical command patterns, and, as a result, enormous social estrangement among the hired hands.

An overhead overload is simply defined as too many chiefs, too few Indians. Doing business with ITT, the Pentagon, and HEW is like a Marx Brothers fire drill. The incredible proliferation, layer-on-layer, of juxtaposed departments, competing baronies, and unaccounted for principalities is a clear indication of an organization cloudy about its objectives.

Giantism is a form of organizational elephantiasis defined simply as "the bigger we are, the better," graphically demonstrated in the late sixties during the merger madness when every CEO had his eyes on the price of his stock when his feet should have been planted firmly on the ground.

Vertical command patterns are typically military and work fine in authoritarian institutions when the information coming topside is accurate. Increasingly, because of giantism, the information is wrong, wrong, wrong. For fifteen years General Motors sat watching 20 per cent of its market dwindle away to the Europeans and the Japanese. And until 1972 computers told the Pentagon that victory was at hand in Indochina.

But millions of new people on the job market, armed with the cultural equipment of the sixties, are forcing change from below in organizations. The civil rights, women, and youth movements in the past decade have shown no sign of abatement, not to mention the increasing clout older people are wielding against corporate America. Exxon, for example, has agreed to rehire scores of older people laid off largely because of age. International Harvester rehired an attractive female assembly line worker dismissed because she was allegedly and invincibly distracting to her male coworkers. Fire and police departments are hiring women.

And all this change must take place in your huge public/private conglomerates because that's where the jobs are.

So changes are coming in these large institutions. The phones are working better in New York City despite an enormous revolution in the character of its work force. The Navy has taken radical steps to make service life more contemporary. The huge conglomerates are decentralizing; there is clearly an "economizing of scale" movement of major proportions quietly revolutionizing business management. These changes were forced on management from below and met reasonable consideration above. Participation between management and line employees is possible and productive, so long as each party doesn't try to "control" the other.

"What do you mean 'control'? I thought managers were paid to control people."

An enormous distance lies between the day a person is hired and the day he is fired or resigns. That distance is not covered by a book this size. An encyclopedia is necessary to catalogue the myriad relationships, conflicts, and dynamics omnipresent in group behavior, authority/subordinacy roles, and individual self-management.

Still, surveying the employment scene, regardless of the organization, one spots parallel corporate cultural patterns: The similarity of occupational behavior in institutions as diverse as the U. S. Army, the Episcopal Church, Dow Chemical, and the AFL-CIO is astonishing.

One of the more obvious similarities is the ubiquity of the "control" factor.

In simple terms, it is the answer to the question, "Who's in charge around here?"

Authority, no matter how invisible or gentle in application, arouses in the hearts and minds of people at every level in an organization the kind of reflexive behavior best understood by family therapists and psychiatrists. Its roots—here I write as the most ignorant of laymen—lie somewhere between our mother's womb and the crib. The acute need for dependence innate in all of us contradicts our healthy lust for independence of behavior exemplified in the adolescent rebellion. People never entirely lose the need for the security our mothers gave us—thus the compelling movement to stay dependent on the corporation for our psychic and physical needs. Many of us never make a wholly satisfactory adjustment in the transition from adolescence to the adult world—thus our childish need to quarrel with the organizations we professedly serve.

Trapped by our needs (that is, an income), which depend on the corporation, on the one hand, and our innate need to be free of the corporation and "independent," on the other, it's no wonder we are all so confused.

This inner conflict finds expression in the push to "control" our environment—either passively submitting to its stimuli, or trying actively, persistently to change it. So whether we try to dominate our surroundings or adjust to them, we feel we must have some "control" over our environment. And since a large part of our work environment in "knowledge" or judgment jobs is *other people,* it follows that we try, vainly, to "control" other people.

Especially able managers are those who cope with their "control" problems. Leadership is understanding, no matter what power we wield inside an organization, regardless of our skill, experience, seniority, status, and title, that we *cannot control other people.* All we do is negotiate, bargain, discuss, disagree, agree, and interact —there is never complete consonant agreement on every issue in the vast area of human relationships. The responsibility of management is to establish organizational objectives on which all members of an organization focus. These objectives are independent of our own psychic confusion. That's why defining and redefining organizational objectives are so terribly important.

"Where I work we constantly restudy how to improve working conditions and improve the economic incentive to perform more productively. Is this an example of trying to 'control' our people?"

Yes, if policy is substituted for face-to-face confrontation.

For openers, and from deep in my head (and the bottom of my heart), here is why:

1. Managers are terrified of human involvement—thrashing out real problems of a personal nature with live human beings. Most managers prefer systems, processes, and procedural policies to govern conduct—this takes the monkey off their back, and the poor, old "system" (once again) is blamed. Thus the grousing in the government cafeterias, troop mess halls, and corporate dining rooms —"I want to do such and such, but the system won't let me."

2. Managers hate to feel they are *not in control.* This might be why they sought line management positions in the first place. It is also the reason most of them fail as managers. Because nobody *can control anything.* I can't control what you think of this book, and you can't control my writing it. I can't control my secretary's time, though I use a thousand stratagems, and she can't control what I will want her to do. I can't know whether the public will want my product tomorrow, and the public can't be sure I'm even going to provide it. *Control,* ladies and gentlemen, trying to make the universe conform to my inner needs, is the neurotic objective of most managers. Thus the management classes reach out for every patent medicine gimmick the business healers can supply. The resulting delusion is not without its compensations: By trying *something,* managers believe they are in *control.* Which is why they adopt these pernicious systems in the first place. Motivational theories, for example.

3. Managers welcome dependency behavior. It proves they *control* people—which management thinks it is paid to do.

Social workers, five years ago, encouraged welfare dependency. It showed they were in control; their neurotic needs to serve people reduced their clients to the very state society professed to deplore. In like manner, managers, while paying lip service to independence and self-reliance, are terribly threatened by its implications and in a thousand actions underwrite systems to emasculate and made dependent (and therefore *control*) their hirelings.

4. Managers hate emotion and love systems. The latter prevents the former. This means no human confrontations or involvement, and thus perpetuates the reign of the computer mentality, the idea that machines, properly programmed, can award merit and promotional increases in pay. Nobody is going to argue with a computer. The systems idea screws you and me and is, therefore, democratic. And this specious democracy, this ill-concealed lust for "fairness" and "equality," robs managers of the power they have a right to exercise of (a) the evaluation of their people and (b) the allocation of unequal pay for unequal work.

"If I can't 'control' people, how can I assign them work?"

No problem.

At 2 A.M. an editor tells a newsman to cover a downtown fire.

A company commander orders a platoon sergeant to take hill No. 609.

The CEO mandates a market research project on the feasibility of selling fridges to Eskimos.

Nobody is trying to control anybody; newspapers print the news, armies fight battles, businesses sell products and services.

The lazy newsman who's resentful at being dragged from the sack, the platoon sergeant angry for having to move on the enemy, and the researcher who prefers building a market model in Greater L.A.—all suffer from control problems of their own. They don't accept the *terms* of their employment or the objectives of the organizations. But they can't control their environment any more than you can. What they can do is change environments (that is, find another job).

But nothing in Scripture prevents them from *discussing how to do the job*. For example, the newsman suggests a photo story, the sergeant advises a dawn attack, the researcher counsels aiming at the urban Aleut market. In a word, all would discuss and participate in the decision and disagree with leadership, if they feel real *conviction*. In fact, that's what they are paid to do.

Managers' "control" problems stem from a congenital inability to brook discussion, participation, involvement, conflict, and resolution. Managers want to see people jump. Not think. Or feel. Or fight.

No way.

"Well, if conviction is good and compromise bad, how does that help resolve conflicts?"

Neither conviction nor compromise, as a value, is good or bad. The best test of someone at work is his attitude toward conflict solutions: Once a verdict is reached, does the person hold the fort or make peace with the posse? What matters is attitude: vainglorious in victory?

Rigid and resentful in defeat?

All bad signs.

Great leaders make mistakes all day. Most institutions make far more business errors than the public or their shareholders ever suspect. Accordingly, how do managers react to defeat, failure, and mistakes? Is it the same attitude they display to success? Far better to zero-in on someone's posture *after* defeat and victory. Is he the same man at Waterloo he was at Austerlitz?

Conflict situations are creative; there are winners and losers. Compromise, consensual group think muffles conflict, and the fires go underground and break out elsewhere another day. That's why fighting on the job is so important. Fires are put out by people who love conviction and hate compromise.

"But won't competent, self-reliant, and independent people threaten my middle managers?"

And maybe some of your top managers, too.

Then fire your weak managers! And if you happen to be so unlucky as to work for an ineffective boss who feels intimidated by your competence, why in the world do you want to work for him?

End the relationship. Quit. Go hire another employer where you are effective.

"Do managers who take risks have control problems?"

Nowhere near as bad as managers who don't.

They know they can't control their environment.

To be successful, take risks—risks with money, plant, product, and people. The reward is prosperity; the worst that can happen is failure —a common enough occasion in most our lives. The greatest entrepreneurs have a history of failure alongside success. A risk taker is a natural leader.

"In hiring managers, look for the risk-taking capacity?"

Yes, but a word of caution.

When filling important jobs, the vast majority of managers portray a job to be more challenging than, in fact, management is prepared to let it become. A fantasy grows in the employer's mind about the challenging aspects of the job; it becomes part of his recruiting pitch. When, in point of fact, what managers really want is someone to *jump*.

"So management or 'managing people for results' doesn't mean controlling them?"

Because so much of our work environment is "other people" and our need to accommodate to this environment at any cost, it follows that people at every level spend a good deal of time and emotional energy trying to *control other people or fighting being controlled by others*. Then the People Problems begin.

It is the People Problems that are the stuff of management. So many people "want work with people." It is the tritest response in any elementary job placement or job-counseling situation.

I gag on its banality.

For if you would work with people (no matter for what type of organization), you are in fact a manager. Women, especially, shy away from management—far more young professional women go to law school than seek admission to business school. But management is, by definition, where the People Problems are. And it's where people with strong predilections for observation, empathy, feeling, and sense of human relationships make an enormous contribution.

"Yes, but isn't there an 'old boys' club' which bars women from important management positions?"

Every woman ten years on the job and ten yards from the goal line thinks so.

And I certainly don't mean a woman must go to business school to become a manager. Most effective male managers, for that matter, don't. But I know for certain that business schools in this country are clamoring for and not finding enough distaff applicants. Any female graduate from a good business school in 1974 can count on twice as many job offers as her male colleagues. While this demand is clearly a result of increased pressure from the federal government, young women are making a big mistake overlooking the advantages of business occupations.

As for the old boys' club, once women do break into management, its continued existence is another example of the "control" problem. Men don't meet at midnight in the boardroom to plot how to keep women from positions of power. But there is no question men, when they think of management, think of men. "Have you thought about hiring a woman for the job, J.B.?" I sometimes say to a client. The pause that precedes J.B.'s answer is pregnant with prejudice. Of course, the idea never passed through his mind. But now it has, thanks to more and more women looking for management jobs.

The major point I want to make to women interested in management is to make them want these jobs *more*. Wanting a job, as we shall see later on, is a major qualification. Secondly, and I don't have to make this point already being made daily by women around the country, is for women to press hard for Top Management jobs. Particularly *inside* the organizations where you are now working. Trying to move in on a Top Management job from the *outside* for a woman is still a rugged and frustrating experience. But inside where you work now, the savvy woman *wanting* management responsibilities can fight for her convictions and break the male hegemony of trying to "control" ascension to the executive suite on the basis of primogeniture.

"But if managers don't try to control people who work for them, won't that cause a lot of conflict, which could lead to chaos?"

Quite the opposite.

Conflict *precedes* an orderly environment. Chaos follows when conflict is *suppressed*. Goldbricking, industrial sabotage, competitive Brownie-pointing, executive backbiting, and all the rest are the results of corporate benignity.

Because nobody likes to be controlled, free expression being the deepest longing of human beings, conflict that is the result of a free expression is as necessary as H_2O. A test of this kind of freedom is how *free* people are within themselves and in institutions to express dissent.

The "control" problem accounts for the perennial hostility between the branches of an organization and its headquarters, between component firms of a conglomerate and the holding company, between the field offices of federal agencies and "Washington." The need for decentralized structures and local decision-making authority is a problem that more and more organizations, to their credit, are learning and adapting to every business day. Management of huge organizations is increasingly becoming the art of delegating the appearance and realities of power to smaller units without giving up the necessity for progress evaluation and *goal-setting*.

The problem that managers have "controlling" institutions is manifested in the constant, comical "reorganizations," seemingly endless, played out after a change in Top Management or when painful personnel decisions can't be faced. HEW has undergone so many "reorganizations" in my lifetime that it has become a farcical textbook in organizational dysfunction.

Too many words have been wasted on a rather minor state of the art known as organizational development, which is the science of how you shape an organization to reach its objectives. Whenever an organization is confused about its goals, it initiates a movement to reorganize the place.

The triumph of form over content.

Organizational development is predetermined by goals. It is an organic and growing thing not lightly tampered with because it expresses institutional personality. Once managers define goals and win over their people to these objectives, they become free of their own control problems. Growth in an organization—like a flaming hibiscus —takes place.

"But doesn't everything you're saying foul up the whole superior/ subordinate relationship?"

A nasty word, subordination.

Like atheism, alienation, extrapolation.

An ugly, ill-human "process" word favored by personnel specialists who treat people as production components and inventory units.

Never refer to anyone who theoretically works "for you" as a *subordinate*.

Not if you are interested in high productivity, morale, and motivation. The very word itself is inappropriate to effective business and decision-making dynamics. It presumes a traditional, hierarchical, nontask-oriented climate of work.

Increasingly, no matter what the organization *does,* the vertical, hierarchical authority pattern is yielding to the lateral, consensual style of leadership. The Gilded Age of heroic leadership is long dead—replaced by the "human relations" school, which finds its symbol in the Organization Man. Providentially, institutions are perceiving the value of conflict, human confrontation, and involvement as improvements on the conformistic, "to get ahead, you go along" mentality. Authority is divided on an appropriate task-oriented basis: Tomorrow you lead, today you follow; for leadership is increasingly functional in task-oriented work environments. Leadership changes and is shared by those who have the specialized knowledge, the "expertise," to cope with the immediate problems and objectives, only to yield leadership tomorrow to other key specialists better able to cope with future problems. Although no one is in complete "control," the boss is still responsible—that is, required to respond to the best judgment available from his staff. That's why independence of judgment is so vital in "subordinates"—why we should pay people plenty to *disagree* with us. Then we are certain to trust their judgment when they agree.

"But isn't my job to goad my best people?"

It's two-way traffic.

Effective people working together provoke excellence in each other: There is the innovation friction of two humans *making fire together.*

So bear down on your people. Nice guys finish last.

And let them bear down on you.

Because every time they test you—and good men and women are a constant goad to excellence—you grow in competence as a manager, you learn from people below you.

And because you know who you are and welcome disagreement, they learn from you.

Result?

People are loyal to you because you admit mistakes, because they can voice their own feelings, because they learn from you. Your line managers "feel free" with you. "I can talk to my boss and he talks back to me" is an extremely high compliment—and the rarest event in the executive suite. Repeated morale surveys support this proposition: People are really loyal to those they feel freest with; any other kind of employee behavior is dependent in nature.

"Do managers manifest their control problems in every on-the-job situation?"

Every manager has a control problem. How well he has it under "control" is a test of how good a manager he is!

Another "law" is at work here: Our ability as managers to feel control varies in direct proportion to the distance of where we are to the person, situation, problem, or event we are trying to control.

I know CEOs who bark out orders to subsidiary division chiefs (and other barons of the realm spread halfway around the world) and literally quake in the presence of their own secretary in assigning an arduous typing chore.

Twenty years in the world of work, and I do believe—no matter the station or rank of most people—that we are *afraid* of each other. That's why we substitute personnel processes for face-to-face problem-solving, why we lay down the law in a memo to "Our Man in Rio" and secretly tremble when our secretary takes umbrage. That's what "human relations" administration has done to most organizations; it turns tigers into tabby cats and Russian wolfhounds into cocker spaniels.

"Should managers program conflict situations into long-standing institutions?"

It takes time, and the place to start is with the kind of people you hire.

Not long ago, back when bread was ten cents a loaf and the Yankees were a shoo-in for the American League pennant, when growth stocks were all the rage and men could say (with a straight face), "Gee, I'm a junior exec at J. C. Penney" . . . back during our age of innocence, there was something called human relations management. It's still a virulent ideology and shows continuous growth curves in Theory X institutions.

My point is: Because we are human, we secretly welcome (or should, if we value our mental health) conflict situations; they are useful and productive and healthy and often fun. Conflict is as much a part of the human condition as the duodenal ulcer or labor/management disputes. So why in the enlightened seventies do we shy away from creative conflict situations, which are preconditions for progress and solutions?

Probably because of something Mother told us. About nice people not fighting and making a scene. But all the nice, *effective* people I know fight like hell—all the time. Ask my wife.

"So People Problems are natural and inevitable concomitants of growth in healthy institutions?"

Imagine institutions that advertise perfect internal harmony among their key people.

Totalitarian governments, for example.

All that accumulated grievance and repressed conflict eventually explodes. The pieces, of course, are put back together again by different people who practice the same *style* of authority as their predecessors. That's the trouble with revolution: The principle of authority remains the same; only the principal actors change.

"Horreur du face-à-face."

That's what the French call the inability to face up to the consequences of association, participation, confrontation, conflict, and resolution.

Effective managers, in hiring key people for judgment jobs, need to focus, therefore, on candidates who have the capacity to make waves, rock the boat, question authority—which is what is meant by the expression "first-rate people hire first-rate people; second-rate people hire third-rate people." Potent people who hire for results welcome a staff where each individual in some areas is *smarter* than the boss. And every observer of organizational leadership marks an effective manager by the people around him.

"All very well and good, but I still like to run a shop where there's harmony among the hired hands."

And so does everyone. But two disharmonic chords together often make a melody. That's what's meant by association, participation, involvement, conflict, and resolution.

People on the job are involved. This means they fight. Conflict. One party loses; the other wins.

Good losers never bear resentment. That's what people who don't fight feel. Harmony is the product of important issues joined openly and resolved.

Small wonder that most American men lie about of a Sunday afternoon saturated in the violence of professional football—because the only exciting thing that will happen tomorrow is his battle for transportation survival on the freeway going to work.

"Isn't this plea for conflict situations an invitation to office politics?"

Just the opposite. The central reason people leave jobs is because of bad politics—that is, people squabbling over other people. Most people call the problem a "personality conflict" or "a breakdown in communications," which are the consequences, not the causes, of a failure in on-the-job relationships.

Whenever a job candidate tells me he isn't interested in such-and-such a position because it's too "political," it's the tipoff that the person is frightened of other human beings, that he is easily intimidated, that he doesn't want a job with people.

No laughing matter.

Most people say they want work with people, and every judgment job is *that*—squared. But what these self-same people can't face is that people and politics are like a horse and carriage—there's no way you can separate the two if you want movement.

CHAPTER 3

Dumb jobs, grunt jobs, nonjobs, and growth jobs

"What exactly is a growth job?"

A growth job:

1. is never permanent.
2. makes you like yourself.
3. is fun.
4. is sometimes tedious, painful, frustrating, monotonous, and at the same time gives a sense of accomplishment.
5. bases compensation on productivity.
6. is complete: One thinks, plans, manages, and is the final judge of one's work.
7. addresses real needs in the world at large—people want what you do because they need it.
8. involves risk-taking.
9. has a few sensible entrance requirements.
10. ends automatically when a task is completed.
11. encourages self-competitive excellence, self-management, and co-operation.
12. causes anxiety because you don't necessarily know what you are doing.
13. is one where you manage time, money, and people, and where you are accountable for specific results, which are evaluated by people you serve (that is, customers, shareholders, taxpayers, students, clients, consumers, etc.).
14. never involves saying "Thank God it's Friday."
15. is where good judgment is the one, maybe the only, job "qualification."
16. is where the over-all objectives of the organization are supported by your work.

17. gives every jobholder the chance to influence, sustain, or change organizational objectives.
18. is when you can quit or be fired at any time.
19. encourages reciprocity and parity between the boss and the bossed.
20. is when we work from a sense of mission and desire, not obligation and duty.

"That's a mouthful. Is there any data base to support your conclusions?"

Nothing but the stories of about ten thousand people I've interviewed in the past ten years.

Not enough work is being done by the industrial engineers, psychologists, and personnel types in telling us whether a job is a good one or a bad chance. In fact, judging from many job descriptions, most jobs seem alike in so many ways, only a born troublemaker like me can spot the shade of difference between *this* job and *that*. So, in order to augment human knowledge, what follows is a modest attempt on my part to help employers and job seekers alike define what in fact we mean by "work."

"Are all these growth jobs superstar positions?"

Oh, sure, the CEO, the departmental chiefs, and so forth.

Growth jobs are not limited to the power house, where the usual job description reads like a Victorian prescription for Empire. But every growth, judgment, or knowledge job is one without which your people are a leaderless horde wandering in the wilderness. These jobs impact on the critical mass of the place. There are never enough judgment-job candidates.

That's why recruiting Mr. or Ms. Pluperfect is the most important thing you are going to do today.

"Are there a lot of these growth jobs around?"

One day a friend said to me, "Dick, can you find me one of those senior-level executive jobs I'm always reading about in *The Wall Street Journal?*"

Well, ten years in the trade and no manager ever phoned and asked for a "senior executive." Or even a junior one.

An utterly meaningless description, useful maybe to business journalists, but hardly an apt description of what a growth job is. What CEOs want when they call is not a "senior executive" but a social programmer, an inventory specialist, a nutritionist—real jobs. And all "senior."

There are far, far more grunt jobs in the world than growth positions. You might occupy a grunt job—I've had two or three. There is a need—an overwhelming need, as a matter of plain fact—in our society to have vastly more grunt than growth jobs.

"So grunt jobs are important?"

For all I know, a bridge toll collector's job is important, although automation surely will eliminate it one day. Similar jobs are necessary, like an elevator operator or a court stenographer. No one with a job like that need feel ill-used—these jobs are responsive to social needs.

Grunt jobs, no matter how low or high the compensation level, are filled with people who labor in the sweat of their face, but rarely out of love for the work to be done. They labor out of a sense of duty ("I've gotta feed the kids, make my mortgage payments, and pay my country club dues"). But people who work in growth jobs find their employment an end in itself—like virtue, its own reward.

"I can't see the difference between a grunt and a dumb job."

There is no "objective" difference.

The distinction is in the mind of the jobholder. If I moonlight as a bridge toll collector to pay for my son's education (he should be so lucky), I have a good grunt job because my objective (sending junior to Podiatry Prep.) provides me the cash to do it.

On the other hand, if I work as a bridge toll collector, hate it, and have no objective except simple survival, I have a dumb job. Plenty of novelists hack for a living: Driving a cab is a grunt job. But the tradeoff for a fiction writer is great; he puts some of his passengers in his next book!

Working in a steno pool is a grunt job; but it can lead into the foyer of the executive suite, *if* my objective is line management. If I have no objective, working in the steno pool is a dumb job.

Stuffing envelopes is a dumb job; if my objective, however, is to elect my unemployed brother-in-law to the City Council and put him on a payroll, then what I've got is a good grunt job.

There is nothing "wrong" about grunt jobs. It sure beats unemployment. And the best jobs in the world can be *dumb* if the jobholder has no inner agenda, no real objective, no reason to work except to eat.

Dumb jobs are their own punishment. We feel "obligated" to work at dumb jobs; we feel "free" to work at growth jobs.

"I don't understand what you mean by 'obligation'?"

I'm *obliged* to labor (I must eat); I'm *free* to work (I must live).

Now, by labor I mean something I'm *obligated* to do. "I labored in the vineyards of the Lord" means you did dumb work that gave you little pleasure (no matter how much lucre you obtained).

This idea of labor was brought to a productive boil by Lord Calvin and the other Swiss theologians who preached that we labor because it is our *duty,* that God's grace anoints those who press the grapes and winnow the chaff. Labor was a pleasure in one sense: It got the awful monkey of obligation off our backs—until we rose again the next morning to fervently welcome another ton of Karma. An endless cycle of labor/obligation, obligation/labor.

This reading of God's will formed the ideological basis for capitalism; it sanctioned wealth, which showed God's grace and signaled our "election" to heaven and eternal life: a good enough reason to labor at a dumb job.

I mean, people really busted ass.

The fact that the Puritan ethic produced guilt in the boxcar was not critically examined until relatively recently; just about the time when our industrial system was making labor even more meaningless and alienated, the religious sanction for labor (labor equals riches and an eternal, heavenly hereafter) was losing force.

Work, on the other hand, is an avocational obsession that just happens to make you a living. There's no obligation (unless, of course, it's in your mind, in which case it is a bad case of "labor" pains). Many successful people hate their work because they are duty-bound. Others, quite "unsuccessful" in monetary terms, love what it is they do. Work is what we *want* to do, not what we must do; it gives us pleasure even though it might cause pain; we work from a sense of mission and not a sense of duty. That's why there are no "careers"—only callings.

I do what I do, not because I must, but because of what I want.

"So there's a difference between labor and work. What do you call a job of labor; a job of work?"

The first is called a *job*.

The second is called a *task*.

That's why in healthy organizations all work is the product of *task forces;* why organizations can't explain themselves via charts and diagrams, which refrigerates, packages, and stores people in neat boxes.

No *task* is *permanent;* all of us, in point of fact, are consultants.

That's right: consultants to organizations for which we work. We stick around so long as a *task* exists for us to *effectively* perform. When the *task* ends, so does our "job"—which means that all of us are unemployed every workday until we identify organizational and personal goals and make them mesh.

For years I have, with some success, tried convincing client firms (including my own) never to hire people—*except as consultants.* That goes for everyone from the production typists to the marketing vice president. The idea works.

People hired as consultants don't develop a hammerlock on a job, never think of it as *permanent,* and stop working the day the task is finished. And are not re-employed until other *tasks* are undertaken.

Make clear to anyone you hire that he is, in fact, a consultant and serves at the pleasure of management and himself so long as a task needs performing—and no longer. Far from discombobulating people, the insecurity, adventure, and realism of the *task* approach to work (as opposed to the job approach) turn people on to you and your organization.

Consultant relationships (like any relationships) can last a lifetime—so long as both parties realize they are unemployed until both agree on goals and the *tasks* to reach those goals.

"Well, if every important job is a consulting relationship, how do you keep up continuity within organizations?"

Some organizations don't need continuity. Others, well, they are largely in business because the key men and women who make the place work stay on while less important people are periodically changed over. It is one thing, at my firm which sells consulting services, to program high turnover; it is altogether another thing—in a petroleum refinery for example—to expect people to work on a task-oriented basis.

The principle is still sound, however. There is relative more job continuity with a petroleum company, for example, because the demand for its product never slackens. The same theory, of course, applies to insurance, food processing, real estate management—all products or services which minister to establish human wants. All the more reason in "safe" employment institutions, like the drug companies or the Social Security Administration, for Top Management to *program* the task-oriented approach, continually to particularize *tasks* (rather than jobs), to overhaul job descriptions (or even eliminate them entirely) so that people feel the bracing winds of change and feel a healthy insecurity. *No matter where anyone works the worst fate is to know your job is for life.* And if you have such a job, the way to make it better is to test whether there isn't another occupation that doesn't really deserve your contributions. It might take a year to identify one or two other "careers," but it will free you from the tyranny of absolute security.

"How can institutions function if they don't impose obligatory tasks on their people?"

They can't.

What they can do—in filling these so-called key growth jobs—is pick men and women who labor for love! I mean it.

People who perform work out of a sense of obligation function much less effectively than those who work out of a sense of pride and accomplishment. Sorting out people, spotting their real talents, and matching against the right job constitute an art form. No matter how practiced you become at finding or filling these jobs, you make mistakes.

In picking line managers, operational chieftains—the barons of the corporate realm—focusing on the motives (rather than the education and experiential background of your candidates) is the key to finding, keeping, turning over, and letting your people *grow*. That's because the people in charge are *growing*.

For the rest—the employees who don't know what they want and, if they do, won't act on this information—constant supervision is required. That's because they are *not* growing on the job, work out of a sense of obligation and fear, and can't put their own feelings first. Which is why they constantly complain about the organization: Its objectives are an *obligation,* which they *resent*.

"I go along with a growth job never being permanent, and I like the idea of it being fun, but how can a job both be fun and at the same time tedious, monotonous, and frustrating?"

• The entrepreneur who takes over shaky businesses and puts them back on their feet.

• The social counselor who works patiently with a school dropout, an alcoholic, or an addict, and sees progress, backsliding, more progress, backsliding, more progress, another step backward.

• The legislative aide who painstakingly nurtures a piece of legislation through hearings, committees, reports, amendments, deletions, more hearings, conference committees, and finally sees it signed into law.

• The stockbroker who patiently builds a small clientele, losing this customer, gaining that one—through bull markets and bear, gradually building a business based on investment instinct.

These jobs—all growth jobs—are tough. Monotonous. Frustrating. The triumph comes in doing the job well, no matter what the outcome.

Some businesses don't make it; some clients aren't rehabilitated; some legislation is never passed; some brokers finally go out of business. The point is not the product of what you do, but the *process*.

All excellence demands pain, tedium, frustration.

A whole generation of Americans (for reasons educators and parents must ponder) has grown up with the childish notion that work must be always "fun." Or, of a liberal cast of mind, "relevant" and, a close second, "meaningful."

The worst result arising from the social upheaval of the sixties (and the attendant Great Society legislation) was the campaign on the part of manpower bureaucrats in Washington to restructure jobs on the basis of what was called "upward mobility."

No more dead-end jobs.

Everyone, particularly the poor, would be given "exciting" (a favorite word of the bureaucrats), "meaningful" work that was "dignified."

New careers.

What the experts forgot was that all labor has inherent dignity, and to say that some jobs don't ("Women are demeaned in secretarial positions, blacks who work as domestics are secondary citizens, etc.") is to perpetuate a gigantic fraud on the presumed beneficiaries of the scores of manpower redevelopment programs to save the lumpenproletariat from an exploitive society.

Bushwa.

"There is no way you can convince me that secretarial and domestic work are good."

A job is neither good nor bad in and of itself. Whether it is a dumb or a grunt job is in the mind of the jobholder. If the government of the United States implies that posthole digging is a bad job, small wonder that millions prefer welfare unemployment to such jobs. And grunt jobs, goddamn it, are dignified, necessary, and important.

A busboy, a busman, and a bushwacker perform essential services—grunt jobs. To put people down because of what they do is an intolerable violation of the human condition.

In the Army, infantrymen are called "grunts," the unintended compliment rear-echelon types always pay people up front.

"Well, don't you think we have a duty to upgrade and enrich jobs?"

No, no, no!

The worst result of our new "fun ethic" in this country is the establishment of such new rules as these:

1. Work should not be painful.
2. My work, which is sloppy, is as good as your work, which is excellent.
3. Uniformity, therefore, of pay and privileges to me is more important than rewarding you with higher pay and more privileges.
4. Any work that is boring, frustrating, or tedious is bad and exploitive.
5. Practice never makes perfect—it's simply a bore.

6. Inspiration is worth more than perspiration.

7. Work must be fun.

What has this philosophy wrought on the social polity?

Thirty-five thousand secretarial positions are open today in New York City largely because clerical work is called scut work, unworthy of educated men and women.

Fourteen million people—twice the population of Switzerland—are on welfare.

A 5 per cent unemployment rate is considered normal despite thousands of jobs never created, which go unfilled for lack of seekers.

Millions on unemployment insurance never bother to look for a job until their benefits are exhausted; the law says they needn't change fields or trade because to do so would violate their freedom.

Thousands of young, restless college graduates, many of whom don't know what they want, inflict themselves on the job market, too proud to do "scut" work while looking for their dream job that doesn't exist. The enormous growth in unhappily unemployed collegians educated, apparently, beyond a capacity to work, is a secret social problem—like wife swapping and glue sniffing. A new "advantaged" proletariat, displaced, impotent, and childish, is reaching out for a thousand cures—mysticism, drugs, communal life styles, gurus.

"Does grunt work prepare people for growth jobs?"

Grunt work schools potential managers in working together with people from every walk of life within the organization. That's why many young people don't want to start out any place else in an organization except the bottom.

This lesson should be taught in the better business and professional schools; then I would feel better about "career education."

Grunt jobs train people to cope with growth positions. That's because every growth job contains a lot of grunt elements.

"O.K. Grunt jobs are better than no jobs. Why do people hate grunt jobs?"

People hate a job because it's dumb. Because they are dumb: They have no real objectives, don't care about themselves, and therefore hate themselves.

People can love grunt jobs. Because they have objectives, care about themselves, and feel self-esteem.

The difference between the two jobs is only in the head of the jobholder.

"But shouldn't management try to upgrade and enrich mechanized jobs?"

This book is restricted to judgment jobs which, by definition, are not routine. What you are talking about are production line jobs in factories or bureaucracies where repetitive and mindless reflex actions are the name of the game.

I've had to supervise people in these kinds of jobs and have had a few myself. Without being at all "expert" in industrial engineering, let me report that the best luck I've had in filling these jobs with good workers is with the retarded or physically disabled. Invariably they are happier, more punctual, thorough, and damn glad to make some productive input to society. My point is that these jobs are important and the smart employer will hire people whose functional level matches the job. Steer clear of locking otherwise able-bodied workers into industrial kinds of jobs. The monotony of the job and the rising expectations of the proletariat work against either party to the transaction being satisfied.

In other kinds of mechanized jobs which I've had to fill, I've had bad luck in trying radically to change the nature of the job, largely because I tried to *please* people by showing a concern for their working conditions. My hunch is that managers would do well to allow people to redefine and upgrade their own jobs. Let *them* take responsibility for their own occupational happiness. Your job is to evaluate their suggestions and act on their wisdom. Trying to impress from the top down new working conditions or objectives with a view to improving a job's content robs an individual of the right and freedom to make his own job better qualitatively. Far better for managers to be receptive to changes the men and women *on the line* make.

"Then why do people hate to work?"

1. They work out of a sense of obligation—not love.
2. They suffered from an "advantaged" childhood.

The people complaining most about bad jobs are products of a middle-class background, educated to expect more from the world than the world is prepared to give. This is rooted in the way we raise children these days (or don't raise them).

Children want independence, but they can't be independent until they learn to live with frustration. Children grow up without learning to live with frustration and become rebels without a cause. Freedom is meaningless because the chains that bind them are forever locked on them by their parents, who want to "protect" them from hard work, pain, tedium, frustration. But children need to cope with these immutable factors before becoming free.

When a person is truly autonomous, a *free-acting,* not a "free thinking" person (of which we have a superabundance in America today), he recognizes, as a hundred generations preceding our own *did,* that the world demands and needs our work, which means our sweat ("No sweat," curiously, is still a favorite expression—as if any job worth doing could be done excellently—without "sweat").

For someone without objectives, *any* job is dumb, where there is no sense of achievement, no personal growth, no frustration met and conquered. And the result is rebellion against the terms of life, like a child who can't tie his shoelaces without learning to overcome a sense of defeat such an act requires. And the rebellion is targeted against adults (anyone over forty), who know that the only meaningful work around involves "sweat."

Let rhetoricians in the women's movement, the trade union flacs, the welfare lobbyists—and the thousands of journalistic liberals who write about "scut" jobs as beneath human dignity—remember that we honor God through work, as a field hand, a dishwasher, or a hod carrier.

There's a good deal to be said for the Maoistic concept of forcing the intellectuals, journalists, and bureaucrats—the Mandarin classes —back to the fields to reap the harvest. Once upon a time the idea was as American as apple pie; but lately, what's left is all over our face.

"So growth jobs are frustrating, too. What's the reward?"

What my Aunt Dot called a "sense of accomplishment."
The Puritan ethic.
"A pretty good ethic," my brother is wont to say. "Better than anything else around."
But the trouble was that the Puritans felt *terrible* when they weren't working! Puritans hate pleasure.

Talking to hundreds of people about jobs, what strikes me about the on-the-job experience is the importance of *achievement* as *the* factor in assessing relative job satisfaction.

Test out your job candidates: Make them describe every job and the one factor they liked *most* about each. Why, ask them, does this one aspect of the job stand out?

I'll bet my "Win with Willkie" button it has something to do with being *tested* on the job and not found wanting, of overcoming odds and accomplishing unexpected results, of occupational growth despite (because of?) adversity.

Every job seeker wants a "challenging" gig.

Without thinking through what that means.

People who hire should insist on every candidate being damn precise on this point. At the same time, ask yourself, as an employer, what the challenges are, what the achievement factor is, in the job you are trying to fill—which means thinking through a job and even changing it so it, in fact, becomes challenging.

Some hints to employers: Stop suffocating your hired hands with good working conditions and outrageous salaries. Start "upgrading" jobs so that a little danger, excitement, and anxiety are inherent in the work. Offer specific challenges that require specific responses. The chances are good that plenty of applicants will "select out" at that point, leaving you with people who really want work in the vineyards of the Lord.

And make damn sure any candidate for a job in your shop understands that:

1. Every job in the place, from the CEO on down, includes plenty of frustration, defeat, and tedium.

2. Every job in your firm can be made into what the jobholder wants if he cares enough about himself and the organization's objectives.

3. That all excellence is a product of pain, practice, and perseverance.

What Grandfather told us—and what, in our haste to give our children all the "advantages," we forgot to teach.

"What do you mean, 'outrageous salaries'?"

I'm all for paying effective people outrageously well.

My point is, without being able to measure a person's productivity, management has no way of knowing whether someone is under- or overpaid. Therefore, instead of investing so much time, money, and people into developing uniform and fair compensation schemes, Top Management would be better advised to spend the same amount developing executive productivity scales. Given the nation's social science, management, and statistical science manpower, there is no reason why most institutions can't figure out what their key people are *worth*. And that's why no one, where you work, will receive exactly the same amount of money as the next person. And compensating people based on real productivity is real "equity." Moreover, establishing executive productivity standards does more to sharpen organizational objectives than any other management exercise.

"What's a nonjob?"

Nonjobs often pay well, carry impressive titles, and provide sybaritic work environments. They are usually occupied by men and women an organization can't use any more (and haven't the gumption to fire). Nonjobs are the fur-lined isolation cells used by Top Management to send their dead weight a message: "Quit or the corporation will murder you with kindness."

Many nonjobs are created in the twinkling of the president's eye, the idea being to shelve "good ole Harry," who can't cut the mustard any more or, for one reason or another, needs to be politically neutralized so other men and women can do what "ole Harry" won't let them do.

It's a sin against Harry, the organization, and everyone who works there.

Why?

Again, nobody wanted the responsibility of telling Harry what the score was, of hurting his feelings. Hurt his feelings?

Kicked upstairs is a punishment far worse than dismissal, which, if done right, leaves both parties with a mutual feeling of respect and dignity. But to be suddenly stripped of all power (and inundated with all its symbols) is to suffer a special kind of occupational death.

Other nonjobs are created accidentally, largely within nonprofit enterprises, which are not responsive to market forces, or in institutions that fail to cost out the high price of nonjobs. Nobody, again, cares enough about the organization to save it some money; nobody wants to finger Dick or Jane who, after all, are Nice People.

"Is this job really necessary?" is a question my boss should ask himself once a month. Nonjobs (like nonevents) are endemic to our society, reinforced by the insidious effects of corporate benignity, the "I'm all right, Jack" syndrome, and the strong penchant of managers to featherbed the executive suite.

Tales of nonjobs are rife—nearly everyone I know has experienced the feeling of going to "work" without the slightest need to do anything. Comparatively, the Chinese water torture is a lark.

"How do you fire the dear old Janes?"

Largely because of the absence of many women in the executive suite, what to do with dear old Jane is hardly a burning subject in the minds of most CEOs. My hunch is that if women make the progress within management's ranks to the degree most women want in the next ten years, the problem of dear old Jane could be epidemic. At any rate, what you don't do, if you are in Top Management, is create a lot of nonjobs for good ole Harry or dear old Jane.

"Still, isn't the problem of older people on the job a lot more complex within organizations than you think?"

Not if older folks are pulling their weight and making a real contribution to the organization. The temptation for those with tenure or protected by seniority status is to rest on their oars and wait to cash in on the organizational pension plan. I can't tell you how many people in their fifties and sixties won't switch out from unhappy job situations because they can't afford to. . . . But I bet it represents a clear plurality of the nation's over-fifty executive work population.

Pension plans were never designed to "trap" people into jobs they don't really want. All the more reason for national legislation that would govern portable pension plans which we carry from job to job, like our Social Security benefits. This kind of system would free older people to stay spry on the job market and leave organizations the option of firing people right up to the time of retirement.

"O.K. But does an organization have an obligation to keep on someone at sixty who should have been fired at forty?"

Of course not. Again, to think so is to victimize everyone: Top Management, whose central responsibility is to measure and encourage high executive productivity; effective executives who must wait until the grim reaper or Father Time works his toll on the older drones in the executive suite; older people themselves who secretly hate the organization on which they are dependent.

Lately, older people have been winning some interesting lawsuits against employers some of whom discharged them a few years short of retirement. Employers who want to be fair and at the same time don't want to be victims of an old people's holdup should concentrate on developing productivity scales that accurately measure an executive's contribution. If it can be clearly shown that good ole Harry or dear old Jane are resting on their oars, the only sensible policy is to discharge them forthwith or raise such a row that the message of Top Management comes through clear.

No one, again, has a "right" to a job. A job is not property, no one has a lien against organizations. And that's true for everyone, older people not excluded.

Because our population will have percentage-wise vastly more older people than ever before, now is the time for all of us, young, middle-aged, and elderly, to work together to protect older people from job bias, developing portable retirement schemes, eliminating mandatory retirement schedules (why should someone sixty-five slink off to his golden years if what he or she is doing is making a real organizational contribution?). Treating older people fairly (or for that matter any class, age group, sex, minority) is to base employment, promotional, and assignment decisions purely on productivity standards openly arrived at, frequently restudied, and always binding.

"How can I tell if I have a nonjob?"

You doodle through a mindless staff meeting, read two dumb memos, draft another, engage in five nonbusiness-related phone calls, linger two hours at lunch in the company cafeteria, check out the price of your company stock, argue with your secretary on the spelling of "antidisestablishmentarianism," engage in one and a half sex fantasies, authorize three unnecessary purchase orders, collect on an expense-account voucher, hit the elevator at four fifty-nine, and on a plane trip the next day, tell your seat companion how good the company has been to you.

"Explain what you mean about a job having a wider social impact."

The Civil Service Commission in Washington has a curious and revealing policy. On snow days—winter days when snow accumulation reaches an inch or two—the Commission announces that "all nonessential personnel" may knock off early.

That's what I mean about social impact. If thousands of federal workers can back off their jobs because their "supervisors" perceive some jobs as nonessential, what a sorry state government has reached. And how miserable to be told your job was nonessential! No wonder government has won such a bad name for itself.

A good job has an effect greater than its definition, a wider implication, an immeasurable but tangible impression on a target population. A teacher, Henry Adams once said, never could be sure where his influence might end. And teaching can be a very good job indeed. There are less obvious occupations that have profound implication for their effect on civilization, everything from an air traffic controller to a food supplier. These are real jobs because they minister to human needs.

"How soon can you tell whether someone is going to work out in a growth or judgment job?"

Nine months is the old ball game: a period of gestation when either something of real issue is brought to birth on the job or its holder aborts. During the honeymoon, the marriage of job and job seeker is given a chance to coalesce, and expectations on the part of both parties—employee and employer—are in suspense.

It is both the best and sometimes the worst of times, because it doesn't take nine months to tell if this marriage can be saved. There are grounds for divorce often within two weeks. But in nine months a manager can be *certain* of the rightness of his choice in filling a job.

"What about the anxiety factor—not necessarily knowing in a growth job what you are doing?"

"Into every life a little rain must fall."

And on the job, everyone runs a little bit scared.

In a good job you don't necessarily know what you are doing! Or how well you are doing.

That's why all first-rate administrators are "crisis managers," why all good infantrymen are "field expedient," why successful marketing types always "fly by the seat of their pants."

If, at work every day, you know exactly what you are going to do and how to do it, then, friends and neighbors, you've got a grunt job.

Anxiety causes the heart to thump and pumps adrenalin into the bloodstream; it teaches the body how to cope, and it is a *sine qua non* in most judgment jobs.

That's why a nonjob is so terrible. The free-floating anxiety factor can't find a subject. There is nothing to *worry* about. That's why people in nonjobs frequently have nervous breakdowns. All that anxiety has nowhere to go.

It's enough to make a man quit his job—which is Top Management's idea.

"What are some examples of growth jobs, now that we know something about them?"

A growth job is one where you hire (and fire) your own people, raise, budget, and spend your own money, take responsibility for a specific task, department, or project, and are evaluated on the basis of performance by people to whom you provide a product or service.

A mouthful.

In a corporation, you manage your own profit center.

In government, you chair a task force with a special mission.

In a foundation, you monitor a program and are responsible for its impact.

In a school, you are judged by your students—did they learn what you taught them?

Simplistic?

Yes, and necessarily so. The chief ingredient in judging whether your job is a growth job is *accountability*. Did you have the action, are you the *responsible* party?

An interesting word, responsibility. It means able to respond, which means the power to act. That's why growth jobs are, in the best sense of the word, political. You want, need, and use power.

Many people shy away from power, believing it corrupts. That's why the same people complain about their jobs. Having power means exercising responsibility, which secretly frightens people who are *unable to respond.*

"But doesn't power corrupt and absolute power corrupt absolutely?"

Power doesn't corrupt—it is irresponsible people who corrupt power. People unable to manage the tools of power—which is to say money, people, and resources—are irresponsible. They are unable to respond—irresponsible.

Absolutely irresponsible people corrupt power absolutely.

Whether you have a judgment job, want one, or are hiring people for such jobs, the most important quality to look for in yourself or in others is this capacity to play politics. That's why leaders in every organization from the Mafia to the Roman Catholic Church are politicians. To avoid politics on the job is to select yourself out of a shot at Top Management.

"Do you really buy people 'playing politics' on the job?"

You bet I do!

What divides us on this point is semantical. My definition of bad politics in the office is the consequences of not playing power politics openly, fighting for your convictions. The result of not trying to assume and exercise more power in your occupational life is to rationalize your "powerlessness" by blaming the "system."

"Don't fight City Hall—an effective woman is never going to be named marketing manager at ABC, Inc.!"

"Sure, what the boss wants done is unethical, but our general counsel says it isn't illegal; why fight it?"

"Sure, Harrison's profit-center is a losing proposition, but he only has four years to retirement."

"Don't spit in the soup, we all have to eat."

The bad name of playing power politics on the job is a result of the human relations orientation which says, "controversial people never get ahead." That's bull. My observations are that *only* controversial people ever deserve or have the competence to be number 1 (or even 2 and 3 in an organization!). Sure, plenty of "controversial" people are "fired"; many "quit" on principle. But people who are prepared to put their job on the line are those who have the confidence of finding another, better job. And they are the real organizational leaders of yesterday, today, and tomorrow.

Now it's true that plenty of people who play bland politics, never look to the right or left, and never make waves—through an organizational homogenization process—do end up their careers as the Top Management person. My impression is that the long road to the top has robbed them of that capacity to make daring decisions, take risks that make organizations grow. That's why in recruiting CEOs I look for this "X" factor in a candidate: the ability to come down hard for his convictions no matter what the consequences.

What most people mean by "playing politics" is quite the opposite of what I mean. Office politics, the worst sort, is guerrilla warfare waged under the cover of indirect discourse, management by memorandum, executive browniepointing, the stiletto between some deserving man or woman's shoulder blades. Most people can spend one hour in most organizations and tell whether people really "like" one another or are jungle fighters in mufti. And this kind of atmosphere is a result of not playing confrontational politics.

"Don't you think it's a lost cause to expect organizations to change their whole personnel structure?"

Organizations won't change unless individuals make them. Don't expect the "system" to change if you don't press your own convictions.

"Lost causes" are the only battles worth fighting.

Christianity, Gaullism, the Copernican theory, and night baseball were once considered "lost causes."

And they all prevailed.

Few people at the outset of their occupational lives find jobs that match up against *every* growth job characteristic. My hope is that people—no matter what their employment stage—will use something like this check list to evaluate the quality of their job. Each job will improve progressively. At the same time, if they hire people (and almost everyone, especially in large organizations, has a hand in the employment process), this same check list can be used to define a job's real scope.

"How does a growth job encourage self-management and co-operation?"

The women's movement has done excellent work cataloguing what the competitive spirit does to men in the marketplace and what it does to women, if they accept the totems and shibboleths of our workaday society.

This kind of behavior, where badges (scholarships, level of earnings, schools attended) are more important than solid accomplishments, what Riesman calls "other-directed," still saturates the American modern-day work ethic. Final authority lies with group opinion and is validated by the competitive pressure to conform. No wonder so many job seekers don't know who they are or what they want.

No, the important point—on the job—is whether a person competes, whether he feels *free* to *compete against himself:* self-management.

To establish, as so many organizations do, competitive standards of performance is to manipulate groups—a neat trick and all the more insidious for being completely totalitarian, and practiced in your best blue-chip firms.

But I do believe that it is within the power of every person to be *free* through self-management, to establish personal indices for on-the-job production, and to be compensated accordingly.

That means *competing against ourselves,* like artists, athletes, true professionals. People who have an inner-directed, autonomous sense of excellence are not dependently in need of group recognition and stimulus. When they fail, they fail in their own eyes, not in the world's; when they succeed, it is against their own standards of internally measured success.

Independent people value co-operation, rather than competition, with one another. Independent, self-managed individuals are free from the need for other-directed and outside stimuli. That's why independent people have no trouble being involved with people: They are neither burdened by the self-protecting ego of the individualist nor manipulated by the competitive pressure of the herd. Independent, self-managed, autonomous, and involved people *want* to co-operate because they are *free.*

"But where I work, competition is the only incentive that keeps the place going!"

People who love their work compete against only themselves.

My choice every time is to keep company men on the shelf, hire some gunners to keep the place alive, show company bullies the door, and go after the people who put their craft, trade, talent, flair—call it what you will—at the organization's service.

No, it's better to have some competition rather than none at all. But if organizations set up executive productivity standards and key people are compensated accordingly, this is an enormous help in aiding everyone to be a "self-manager." From that point on, you measure progress—not against your peers—but against your "record." From thenceforward, you are competing against yourself. For some people, who need the goad of peer pressure, this system doesn't work *at first*. But given time and an alteration in priorities, excessively competitive people find out it's more fun.

"What do you mean by every growth job having a few sensible entrance requirements?"

Every good, judgment job has low entrance requirements. Whether looking for a growth job or trying to fill one, therefore, you can expect the requirements, the "criteria," to be simplified and reduced the more important the job.

Let's take the headquarters of American bureaucracy: the State Department, the original fudge factory. A Foreign Service officer must pass a rigorous written examination, an oral panel review, a security clearance, and compete in rank on "a list" before being appointed FSO-8 at the munificent sum of $9,200 per year. The Secretary of State, his boss, only need survive a favorable interview with the President of the United States, a security clearance, and usually routine confirmation by the Senate before being appointed.

Which is the better job?

Another illustration:

The President of the United States must be a citizen and thirty-five years or older. There are no other "requirements." Contrast this, the most important job in the country, with, let's say, your job!

Twelve years ago, the Peace Corps needed to make a crucial policy decision: What "qualifications" were needed for someone to work effectively overseas?

The first policy proposal was: any American eighteen years old or older and recommended by five citizens. Some argued for a second proposal: that a foreign language was a *sine qua non,* a university degree, overseas experience, a licensed "trade," and so on. . . .

The first course was adopted. And the Peace Corps, along with the Metroliner and the space program, were damn near the only government programs that worked in the sixties. Had the second course been adopted, we can be sure the Peace Corps would have foundered.

"Then why do employers establish all of these nit-picking entrance requirements?"

The labor union mentality.

Bad jobs are notoriously protected by a thicket of regulations. Hard to qualify for, these jobs are stupefyingly secure once all the hurdles are jumped. Security, not only of income, but security of *place:* Your status in our society is established by *what you do.* It's the most frequent question asked of you at a cocktail party. "What do you do for a living?" And that goes for your friendships and social life, most of which are governed by what you do.

Job, income, and "social" security is the objective of protected occupations.

"You are surely not saying that growth jobs don't require any qualifications at all?"

No, indeed.

Some requirements are necessary—I want the man or woman who takes out my appendix to be a certified, graduated, board-diplomed surgeon.

The point, of course, is not to confuse yourself, whether you are looking to fill a growth job or qualify for one, by focusing on nonessentials. While it's true the best and most powerful jobs in our society lack the host of qualifications we burden most jobs with, it is also truer that finding the top men or women to lead in our society is increasingly difficult. The reasons are that most people are afraid of leadership positions these days; authority figures are not exactly popular figures. That's why developing a talent for controversy, fighting for your convictions, welcoming visibility in leadership jobs are central factors in being picked up for a top job.

"So the most important jobs in our society have the least qualifications. There must, however, be a thousand candidates for these jobs."

One of the more interesting things, as a headhunter, I've learned about the employment process is the unusual number of solid, well-paid, and responsible positions open at any one time. In good times and bad, there is always a need for effective people. Contrary to the conventional wisdom, the hardest jobs to fill are growth jobs. What is scarce in the employment mart is not good jobs, but people to fill them.

This is no idle observation.

People, effective people at every level, are what are hard to find.

"Aren't you being awfully simplistic?"

The next chapter should clear the air.

My point here is that if you employ people, try reducing the job down to its quintessential elements, eliminate as many fixed qualifications as possible.

This frees you to find the most *effective* people to fill your job; not necessarily the *most qualified*. The difference between the two groups is the distinction we see between growing and failing organizations.

CHAPTER 4

Matchmaking

"Hire people's strengths—not their weaknesses; sounds easy, but is it?"

Peter Drucker, in his excellent book *The Effective Executive,* retells a story I've repeated a dozen times around the country. About Abraham Lincoln's management problems during the Civil War—his search for a general.

Lincoln churned practically the whole Union Army General Staff before finding his right man. There were Pope and Meade and Burnside and McClellan and others. All his generals checked out: graduates of West Point, excellent performance ratings, combat experience (the Mexican War): All passed muster. But none turned around the Army of the Potomac and marched South.

A sad tale, repeated many times in hundreds of institutions from universities to corporations to government organizations every year.

The right man eludes.

And modern-day institutions—like the Union Army—whip through a succession of superstar commanders (directors, presidents, chief executive officers), making headhunters rich and the public sorry.

What is the moral, as my sixth-grade teacher was wont to say, of this tale? Well, the moral is that management doesn't usually know what it wants.

Abe Lincoln initially picked his generals on the basis of credentials, "qualifications."

The problem with all these carefully hand-picked generals was that they lacked that flair necessary in a wartime commander: aggressiveness. All were interested in protecting the Army of the Potomac (and their own reputations) rather than in engaging Lee.

Finally, in desperation, Lincoln turned to the one commander who fit. Lincoln named Ulysses S. Grant to command the Army of the Potomac.

And who was Grant?

An undistinguished graduate of West Point, a lackluster quartermaster captain in the Mexican War, voluntarily retired at an early age to return to Illinois to indifferently manage a country store, and then recruited by the state militia in Illinois (not the Regular Army) at the outbreak of the War Between the States.

As a battlefield commander, Grant was a success—but only in the sideshow war with Lee's Army in the West. Grant liked his brandy; he was uncouth, possessed none of the social graces, and was far from well-connected in the corridors of power. In a word, Grant wasn't an attractive job candidate except in one crucial sense: He had a habit of fighting.

So Grant became commander of the Army of the Potomac; mobilized the superior armaments, materials, and manpower of the North; and marched his Army toward Richmond. He was defeated and defeated again, but then, through the sheer weight of material superiority, he broke Lee's forces and ended the war a year later at Appomattox Court House.

A grand story.

A grateful nation made him President, the electorate being more miserably endowed with prescience in the people-picking business than was Lincoln. Grant was the worst President in American history (although a couple of recent examples are competing for this dubious achievement award). The Peter Principle, unknown a hundred years ago, found its application in Grant's election: He was promoted to his level of incompetence. Everything that made him a great general conspired to ruin him and his Administration as President.

Sic transit gloria.

But we were talking about the moral of this tale, remember. And at the risk of simplifying the whole story for those readers who still read with their lips, let me sum up and say that nobody, neither the mailroom attendant nor the supreme Allied commander, should be chosen for a job based on nonessentials: the so-called fail factors.

"I'm sorry, but you lost me back at Appomattox Court House."

What I'm trying to say is:

   1. Analyze what a job really requires.

   2. Hire someone who has the talent.

   3. Don't hire anyone for the additional niceties; these are "desirable" attributes, never essential.

Finding talent to fill growth jobs is hard enough without asking candidates to be all things to all people.

"Recruiting for people's strengths is fine, but I always go for the jugular and probe for their weaknesses."

Which is about as easy as banging a spade against a big, red barn.

Ask someone to list their weaknesses and they'll spend the next decade filling out blue books.

But nobody focuses on his strengths, where he is competent, his talent.

This is true for employers as well as job applicants. Employers confuse a job's real definition by augmenting it with altogether too many nonessential redundancies, sometimes completely obscuring the essence of *what it is that needs to be done*. Job applicants, doing an inventory of their background, include a host of detail that rarely wholly supports the job they want.

The result is a blurred photograph of what is needed in a job *and* a job applicant.

"What do you call the one or two quintessential conditions that must be satisfied to fill a judgment job?"

People who hire confuse the issue by specifying a whole series of irrelevant (but desirable) characteristics that make the people-picking harder than it should be.

Now, in Grant's case, the main quality Lincoln wanted in a general was aggressiveness. Nothing else really mattered. The same is true for every job you *fill*. One characteristic, sometimes two, never more than three, are absolutely vital in satisfying the real demands of an important job. Job descriptions, with their hopeless muddle of peripheral and nonessential requirements, never highlight the *one* supremely important factor without which no candidate should be considered. The job of management, yes, and the job of those looking to hire themselves out, is to identify this factor. For purposes of this exegesis, let's call it the flair factor.

"Flair factor?"

That vital talent, skill, capacity, orientation, or ineffable intangible without which no candidate—no matter how well recommended or otherwise qualified—can succeed on the job.

Let me list two columns, the job title on the left, the quintessential flair factor on the right.

The Job	Flair Factor
College president	Accomplished fund-raiser and grantsman
Production typist	150 wpm whiz
Investigative reporter	Persistent, nosy, nattering nabob
Entrepreneur	A risk-taker with someone else's money
Television anchorman	A show biz somebody
Lobbyist	Intelligence-gathering gossip
Contracts negotiator	An Arab in Dacron polyester
Salesman	All alone with nothing but my silver voice and my sample box
Politician	Affably mendacious mendicant

I jest?

Not a whit: Every institution has a classification and assignment clerk, a cosmetician paid to conceal the real essence of any job. The first function of someone who hires is to ignore his job description and, like a laser beam, focus on *what must be done*. That means a gloves-off, unflattering distillation of a job. Focus on the flair factors a job candidate requires.

Make management focus on those one or two qualities. Then you eliminate the vast majority of people really "unqualified" for the job.

In real life, because management does not focus, or does not know what it wants or is confused about what it wants, a whole slew of bad candidates (bad, that is, from the point of view filling the job) are passed through a series of lugubrious interviews, with no one precisely sure (least of all the candidates themselves) as to what is wanted. Because management (read, search committee, the production chief, the chairman of the Board—the hiring authority) did not face up to what they really want. The result is a failure of imagination and the continued stagnation, bankruptcy, and regression of the organization.

"You're putting me on again."

O.K.

Let's go back and look at these same jobs. Without the flair factors. Read the list of qualifications for the job as a classification officer in your firm would phrase it:

The Job	Qualifications
College president	A Ph.D. with five years educational administration experience and an equal number of years' university teaching within accredited institutions of higher learning. Demonstrated publications record. Successful candidates must be married. It is also desirable that . . .
Production typist	Five years' experience as a steno-typist, written recommendations of her proficiency, be of attractive appearance and cheerful disposition. Graduation from an approved secretarial school essential. It is desirable but not mandatory that she have a bachelor's degree and . . .
Investigative reporter	All candidates must be *cum laude* graduates of recognized schools of journalism, have five years' major metropolitan newspaper experience, possess writing samples reflecting an urban studies orientation. It is desirable that . . .
Entrepreneur	Five years' demonstrated success with major blue-chip industrial firm marketing point-of-sale tangibles. M.A. in business administration mandatory. Strong on-the-job experience managing large sales force. Desirable successful candidates

The Job	*Qualifications*
	also have records of civic participation and . . .
Television anchorman	Five years' talent on-camera in major market arena necessary. Combination of writing, producing, and marketing network programs essential. Video-tapes must be provided. Desirable that candidates have advanced degrees in international relations and . . .
Lobbyist	Advanced degree in political science, five years' experience representing trade, manufacturing, or industrial concern in Washington, D.C. Desirable that candidates have worked in legislative/executive branches for no less than three years and . . .
Contracts negotiator	Fifteen years' government contracting experience with major federal agency, strong emphasis on defense-oriented hardware. Only certified CPAs need apply. Desirable that candidates have worked in the Defense Department and/or served as a commissioned officer . . .
Salesman	No less than ten years' experience as a manufacturer's representative in the mid-Atlantic region. Must demonstrate sales leadership potential, prove an annual commission income of no less than fifty thousand dollars, and possess an M.A. degree or its equivalent from an accredited business school. Desirable that candidates . . .
Politician	Democratic Committee is recruiting for a proven vote-getter in the Sixth District to run for state assemblyman. Loyal party men only need apply. Native Virginians preferred. Desirable that candidates . . .

I'm not putting you on!

Maybe just a little bit. I've read as bad or worse job notices for the past ten years.

Does anyone twenty-one or over believe that any of the above organizations have a snowball's chance in hell of recruiting the *right* person for the jobs they have open? If so, I reserve the right to interview the candidates, all one or two of them, before finally passing judgment on the classification function where you work!

"Well, it looks easy, but I think you're still putting me on."

O.K.

Let's take the same list and let me substitute the fail factor, the irrelevant characteristic for which a person was hired.

The Job	Fail Factor
College president	Leading authority on the process of photosynthesis
Production typist	Cute, and laugh a minute
Investigative reporter	*Cum laude* graduate from the Columbia School of Journalism
Entrepreneur	Highest-paid marketing man in the semiconductor industry
Television anchorman	Newspaper gossip columnist
Lobbyist	Ph.D. in political science
Contracts negotiator	Top government program officer
Salesman	Five years' successful purchasing officer experience
Politician	Former director of the Ethical Cultural League of Williamsburg, Virginia

All of these factors *seem* to fit. But, in point of fact, not one of these characteristics is vital and some, as we say at the Defense Department, are "counterproductive."

"What happened to these mismatches?"

I've heard a few thousand explanations about why the last man or woman didn't work out. Let's listen to the client talk:

The Job	*The Client Speaks*
College president	"Dr. Morrison was a grand person and a leader in her field, but the moneybags among our alumni thought she was the widow of the Unknown Soldier."
Production typist	"Betty is the best lunch companion in the office; but why didn't someone give her a typing test?"
Investigative reporter	"Carl? Nice guy. Great on rewrite, but a bummer with people. In six months, he interviewed one person: a highway patrolman who *swore* he saw a flying water bed."
Entrepreneur	"Well, we had to sack him after he bought a company jet and started surveying marketing possibilities in Bangkok."
Television anchorman	"Well, Jack was a knockout print columnist. I wonder why he put people off on the tube?"
Lobbyist	"And to think Walter was a Ph.D. government major; he just hated hobnobbing with all those politicians."
Contracts negotiator	"I never could understand why Martha bombed. She was such a nice person— our contractors were pleased, *but the agency had a 25 per cent overrun.*"
Salesman	"Mac who?"
Politician	"Good old Sam—never told a lie in his life. Quietest campaign I've ever run."

That's the kind of conversations I've had with employers for ten years. Educators call it a "learning experience."

Except, many employers never learn. They go on repeating their mistakes the rest of their lives; like the many job seekers who habitually follow career paths they hate.

Moral: People don't know what they want.

Identifying job objectives.

Defining goals.

This is the chief responsibility of organizations and individuals. Every day, a CEO where you work should ask himself, "What the hell do we *do* around here?"

Every day, people who work for this man or woman should be saying, "What is my job . . . what am I here for?"

"But I thought everyone was hired on the basis of their education, degrees, licenses, previous experience—their qualifications."

That's why two out of three important employment choices boomerang.

People are hired for the wrong reasons. Degrees, pedigree, and previous experience are fine, but they don't necessarily fit what's wanted.

Like Lincoln, employers are mesmerized by nonessentials: superb recommendations, credentials fit for the royal family, educational credits galore. But they don't answer the questions "What the hell do we want this man to *do,* and can he do it?"

Try boiling down the flair factor definition to twenty-five words or less, and question every characteristic your personnel people or your boss (or his) has indicated is important. As the party responsible, as the hiring authority, your job is to keep your eye on the ball while everyone else has his on the Goodyear blimp. The quality you need most in hiring people is ruthlessness, a fine, impartial, clinical objectivity about the real, often hidden, function of a job. Look for the flair factor.

For those of you who like the nomenclature of management science, let's call this theorem the "Functional Theory of Job Placement." "What is this guy going to do?" is the first question my boss should ask me before I bring somebody on board. If I can't answer it, if I give a Chinese answer, the chances are good that I haven't thought hard enough about what is wanted.

"Function" is the key word. What is it that needs doing? Whether you are trying to find a packaging engineer or the next Secretary of State, focusing on a simple definition of what is to be done is the first order of business.

"Don't most employers still hire people based on the experience factor?"

That's why two thirds of their key job placements go *kaput*.

Think about it: How many jobs have you had where you lacked strict qualifications, no "hard skills" but for which you were hired? How did your work compare to that of "experienced" hands?

Think harder: Who would be working today *at any task* if the experience edict applied *universally?* Nobody.

"We can't send those young volunteers overseas—they have no experience."

"We can't send this infantry battalion into battle—it has no combat record."

"We can't send this gal to the sales conference—she hasn't sold anything."

"This person can't teach—she has no experience."

And on, and on, and on . . .

One of the characteristics of a growth job, remember, is not knowing entirely what you are going to do every day you come to work. That's the challenge! Why people *like* to work, why every day is an adventure. Experienced people can become jaded; their work is prefigured by previous experience—they don't bring new ideas, perceptions, or enthusiasm to what they do.

In choosing people for growth jobs, don't, for heaven's sake, dismiss the experience factor. But when five people have a shot at a job and four have the experience and the fifth hasn't and the last candidate somehow is the most impressive in work history, interview presentation, and checkout, in the name of good sense act on your *instincts*. Fight for your convictions. The chances are very good that two thirds of your manpower decisions thenceforth will be right on target.

"If two out of three selection decisions are wrong, what are the chances of improving that ratio?"

For any judgment job, the chance of your making the right selection just because you are a bright person who knows his business is about one in three. Shocking odds? Hardly. To be successful, whether you are managing a signal corps battalion, a university, or a stem-winding conglomerate, I wager that only one third of your decisions need to be the "right" ones. The same goes for hiring. But the aim of this book is to increase your batting average in the people-selection department.

Remember, our focus is restricted to judgment jobs; technicians, production workers, and support staff, while comprising the major portion of the work force quantitatively, are still a minor segment qualitatively. Our society, through the working of market forces, is extraordinarily successful at generating the technicians needed to man the machines; but we seem no better than other societies in finding the ablest men and women to manage the people who manage the machines. In plain fact, good people are hard to find, and finding them should involve a major investment of your financial and imaginative resources—not to mention a good deal of your time.

"Yes, but there still is no substitute for experience!"

I'm not knocking experience.

The electrical engineer with an M.S., five years with GE's light turbine division, and ambitious to work into nuclear power generation is the kind of candidate you want to help your firm design a modern power facility in the Red River Valley.

What I'm saying is that the electrical engineer whose hidden agenda is to work into sales, stay in the Chicago area, and eventually go into the electrical contracting business with his brother-in-law is a bad bet for any company to promote into a responsible operating engineer capacity far from his Chicago home. It's not what he really wants to do.

Far better to go with that electrical engineer with only a B.S., two years' experience, a demonstrated performance record, and an insane desire to move in on the ground floor of nuclear power generation. His motives, damnit, are his "qualifications"—far more than his degree, years in service, or standing in the company.

Another reason why a good man or woman is hard to find. As Mr. Lincoln found out in 1864.

"O.K. Experience is important if it's married to motivation. What about educational background?"

Gather around, children, and let me tell you dark things about higher education that pedagogues admit only to themselves late at night in the faculty club:

The vast majority of college graduates don't know what they want to do; that's why so many go to graduate school.

Educating people for "careers" is a bust. At this writing, I wager that 50 per cent of West Point/Annapolis/Air Force Academy graduates will have donned civvies after five years in the armed forces; 65 per cent of the lawyers graduated each year won't ever practice law; many medical doctors avoid "hands on" medicine; most international relations majors won't relate internationally; public administration majors will take jobs as insurance agents; and business majors will spin off into philanthropy.

Again, the motives, the hidden agendas, the flair factors of millions of college graduates are a mystery to the educator and educated alike, career counseling being based on the *availability* of jobs and not on what the kids *want*.

So in evaluating educational background, look behind the degree, to the candidate's motives. Then make a judgment on how well-educated the candidate really is: Can he read, write, think, and express himself? Which is the main job of education.

What was his standing in his graduating class?

Did he work his way through college?

Was he corrupted by multiple-choice tests, the "curve" theory of grading, the pass/fail idiocy?

Sure, education still means something. Graduating in the top ten at Harvard Law, or *cum laude* from an institution that still *fails* students, or making the dean's list in non-Henney Penney colleges is a big plus in separating out those who know we are *evaluated, graded, and tested* every working day of our lives. Graduates from the other kind of "free" and open institutions are suspect at once. Long on feeling, they are short on thought; grand aspirations and few achievements; snow-blind idealists and gossamer intellects—what these job candidates need is an "education"!

Finding educated people is half right and half wrong.

Better to find educated and *willing* candidates, which is longer and harder.

"Can't the personnel people help?"

Personnel people who write job descriptions base them on the "qualifications" of the *past* incumbent in the job.

Today, all over America, important jobs will be settled by men and women saying "but this man is far more experienced." Or because of his three degrees in advanced mathematical theory. Not bad criteria, on the whole, if you're choosing faculty types, but otherwise an invitation to organizational hardening of the arteries. Accordingly, personnel people take into account "qualifications" of past jobholders (that is, degrees, years of experience, etc.) and formalize these into programmed job requirements. The result: a perfect photograph of the current occupant of the job. And his replacement is chosen, not on how he or she uniquely differs from the previous jobholder (and, by extension, on the *sui generis* contribution he or she could make), but on how he or she replicates the incumbent jobholder.

"O.K., don't let the personnel people write my job description; how do I avoid making the same mistake of photographing myself for a job?"

1. Rethink the job so that its quintessentials, the flair factors, are the sole bases on which a job search is organized.

2. Unless absolutely mandatory, exclude education and experiential criteria.

The key word is "function." What is the function of the person who fills the job? Does he or she scrape the ice between periods at the Rangers' games? Hold the red flag at a construction site? Cost account for the corporation's sinking fund? Plot atomic attack on foreign enemies? Work out mathematical equations to prove out a "two tier market"?

What, sir, is this person going to do?

Often an employer is unconsciously more interested in what a person "is" rather than what he "does," or rationalizes a host of insignificant and nongermane factors into a candidate profile that fits admission standards of a country club but that is woefully inadequate for a particular job.

"Is that how we make the foolish mistakes of hiring people with the wrong 'qualifications'?"

Is the job to market engineering equipment in Africa?

Then why the heavy emphasis on a person's military record?

Don't ask me; ask the man who does the hiring. Ask those hard questions.

This penchant for the irrelevant is common. It sometimes emanates from a hidden agenda to hire a companion rather than an employee. All a prospective job candidate must do is fit some irrelevant fail factors, be likable in the job interview, and before you can say "Jack Sprat," he has the job.

Liking a job candidate is O.K. But why not make a habit of liking *effective* people when you fill a job?

"How can I make myself stop picking likable people and start picking effective people?"

Define the objectives of your job and the flair factors required of a job candidate. Ruthlessly stick to this definition. Let any candidate you want to hire survive a series of interviews with disparate personalities elsewhere in the organization—the kind of people who know your biases, hidden agendas, personal eccentricities, and drinking habits; the kind of people who feel free with you and like telling you the truth. That way you become more effective yourself.

"I still think it's better to recruit all-purpose candidates for an organization focusing on intelligence, flexibility, creativity, and other desirable traits."

That's a great policy for firms doing business in the Italian city-states in the sixteenth century.

But this is the twentieth century, and men and women today are fragmented, alienated, specialized, and suffering from the worst throes of future shock. There are no *integrated* men and women now. That might be the trouble with civilization today. Trying to *grasp* the problem is a feat these days, much less actually addressing and *solving* it.

Hiring on the bases of character traits, personality inventories, and value systems is not working. It's the reason two out of three important hiring decisions abort—and the reason the Peter Principle flourishes.

Far better to treat each employment decision separately—using candidates from any source, specialty, way of life, age bracket, sex, or nationality category. Effective men and women are hard to find. Looking for the all-purpose candidate dooms you to disappointment.

"The whole approach still seems simplistic to me. What happens, for example, when your candidate satisfies two or three quintessentials, he's hired, does a great job, and the flair factors change?"

In other words, the objective conditions of the job change because goals change.

This happens all the time. That's why there is such cyclonic turnover in important jobs, why smart jobholders learn how to change jobs, and why growth organizations always recycle denizens of the executive suite—particularly the top man or woman. Five years is the maximum span most chief executive officers can expect to be effective on the job.

General Grant was the right man at the right place at the right time with the right "qualification." Five years later he was clearly the wrong man, at the wrong place, at the wrong time with the wrong qualifications.

That's why you're lunatic to hire out *anyone* on a contract basis. Organizations commit *hara-kiri* when they lock a superstar into a five-year contract. Nine months later the organization buys him out and then repeats the same mistake. Stick to the Alston principle.

No job in the Western world is as hazardous, from an occupational longevity viewpoint, as that of a major league baseball manager. Walter Alston has managed the Los Angeles Dodgers for twenty-one years! *Never,* repeat, never would he agree to anything more than a one (1)-year contract. Take a gander at the sports pages and see where the Dodgers stand in their division.

"Is setting goals—managing by objectives—as important for people as for organizations?"

Boeing makes airplanes, Dr. Pepper makes soft drinks, Harvard College makes university graduates, and the Federal Reserve Board makes monetary policy. Trouble starts when Boeing starts making golf carts, Dr. Pepper sinks oil wells in the North Sea, Harvard buys a hockey franchise, and the FRB advises the North Atlantic Treaty Organization.

Organizations are changing all the time. And so are people:

- A national park company transits into a vernal Disneyland.
- In the Army, a dump truck battalion is phased into an underwater demolition special unit.
- A management consulting firm in the human services field subtly changes into a social science research organization.
- A government agency in international development changes into a people-to-people exchange program.
- A topflight typewriter manufacturer moves into the computer hardware arena.

People are also changing all the time:

- A practicing oral surgeon becomes a racetrack entrepreneur.
- A combat Marine officer studies arms control.
- An investment banker goes into horticulture.
- A former Episcopal minister transits into hospital administration.
- A literary agent recycles into an English professor.

What happens is that the *relationship* between individual and institution must change or terminate, because *goals* of one or the other or both have changed. Trouble starts when neither party admits that goals are changing; "business as usual." Jobholders need to stay in touch with their own feelings; managers need to know what those feelings are. Which means people must understand organizations, and managers need to get on the side of individuals. Which is management by subjectives.

"Yes, but can't outstanding people cope and change with new conditions?"

Yes, so long as people are not *guaranteed* a permanent job. Otherwise, there is no *need* for them to change, no incentive. Objective conditions change and they don't. Let's look at our jobs again to see what we mean. Objective conditions are no longer the same, but the people are.

The Job	New Conditions
College president	Facultywide strike shuts down institution. State aid to be ended.

The Job	New Conditions
	College prez under withering regents attack. Students march on state capitol.
Production typist	Stenographic Services is wiped out. Each manager assigned individual secretary. Customer complaint chief requires extraordinary tact from staff; light typing load.
Investigative reporter	New publisher to remake Gotham *Blitz* into respectable afternoon financial daily. Crackerjack investigating team's first assignment is to summarize the annual reports of fifty companies.
Entrepreneur	Spectacular sales growth convinces chemical combine to buy out local research lab. Nationwide franchise operation "New Labs, Inc.," envisaged.
Television anchorman	Continued decline in morning viewership convinces network execs to radically change current program format and go with an exciting, new soap opera for the whole family, "The Watergate Waltons."
Lobbyist	National board adopts resolution to censure North Vietnam for continued aggression on its neighbors; Washington representative, a veteran of the '67 march on the Pentagon, asked to hold press conference.
Contracts negotiator	Deputy agency chief orders Contracts Division to expedite at original contractor cost estimates all pending business before November election.
Salesman	New sales quotas for diet cola company announced. West Virginia territory quota increased 15 per cent. Census Bureau announces that eight states suffer from net population loss: West Virginia is third on the list.

The Job	New Conditions
Politician	State convention adopts plank in party platform requiring all candidates for public office to reveal income tax returns for past ten years. Incumbent Fourth District congressman retires "in order to spend more time with my family."

Winds of change.

The *mission* changes with corresponding change in the formal goals of the people who do the work.

Hired to be a company training director, a chap a year later finds himself developing investment strategies for institutional accounts. Hired to do one thing, he ends up doing another.

Determine whether your key people want a new assignment, or find others who do. This implies extraordinary executive turn-over. But it's worth the trade-off in dollars and cents, for, as we learned, there is no substitute for enthusiasm. The most important qualification for a job is hiring a person who really *wants* it. And if priorities are reordered in your organization, a complete overhaul of your personnel structure is necessary to take into account the flair factors and goals of those doing the work.

Now, in the best of institutions, job definitions change overnight:

- A new president turns the company in another direction.
- *This* division is closed to provide resources for *that* department.
- The government contract your firm had last week is canceled unilaterally.
- A lawsuit roadblocks further progress down this corporate highway.

And so on, on, on . . .

There is no end to it. Change, constant change, gives planners acute gas pains, reduces strong men to blue language and beautiful women to fine anger.

"O.K. So jobs go sour on people because of events. But I've hired plenty of people who go sour, and objective conditions at work haven't changed."

That's what I mean by organizations *and* people changing all the time.

Why you, as a people person, need to stay *au courant* with the hidden agendas of the people who work for you. People are changing all the time. That's why you start reading books on motivation. But I can't motivate you (nor you, me) any more than I can control you (or you, me).

Let's review these same jobs again, not from the point of view of the organizations' new objectives, but from an individual's hidden agenda.

The Job	*Incumbent's Hidden Agenda*
College president	Wishes to adapt novel fund-raising techniques to finance establishment of international university in Lübeck, West Germany.
Production typist	Desires transfer to West Coast branch of organization to be near her hospitalized Viet vet brother.
Investigative reporter	Inclined to six-month leave of absence to write up book-length exposé of the diet fad industry.
Entrepreneur	Desires to sell out to national conglomerate, take his profits and invest in air freight scheme.
Television anchorman	Leaning to be a press secretary for national political figure thought to be running for President.
Lobbyist	Penchant toward doubling his income and free-lance representing several noncompeting industries in Washington.
Contracts negotiator	Secretly is negotiating big job with huge aircraft manufacturer.
Salesman	Covets Minneapolis territory, which local sales manager is not exploiting.
Politician	Fancies being appointed the next ambassador to the Court of St. James's.

"So to be a savvy matchmaker, the good manager needs to identify his own objectives and probe to find the usually hidden job agenda of his best candidates?"

Half right.

Knowing what both parties *want* is vitally important. But no less important is weighing whether your best candidates have the *ability* to fulfill their objectives. It's all very well for me, as a job candidate, to want to fly the company's LearJet—the problem is that I've never been checked out for night flying. And, in like manner, an employer who thinks that his job requires a medium-level statistician could monkey-wrench his whole project if what is needed is a Ph.D. econometrician.

No, people-picking is a tough, subjective, imaginative, irrational, and chancy business. And always will be. Because people's hidden objectives must be consonant with organizational goals. And since there is no perfect congruence between the two (any more than there can be perfect adjustment between man and his environment), management problems will exist at least until the next Ice Age.

"O.K. Judging people for jobs means finding out what they want and what they can do. Why is wanting a job so important?"

Without focusing on this matter of *desire,* failing to take into account your candidate's self-interest, and being blitzed by heavy educational or experiential "qualifications" is misunderstanding your candidate's real motives: "What does this person want and why?"

My work with job seekers supports how difficult this question really is. How we admire the person who "knows what he wants"! Less understood, but just as admirable, is the employer who knows what he needs. Rare.

"Why are job seekers so confused?"

Well, in the job seeker's case he looks for a job that is *available.* Not what he wants, but what society provides.

Every trend in occupational preference bears this out. For example, a few years ago the word went forth that there was a shortage of accountants, finance types, and, lo, the business schools are graduating them *en masse*. The year before *that* it was lawyers . . . and before that it was teachers . . . and before that it was space engineers. Next year we are going to be swamped with economists.

"Career opportunity" specialists are hopelessly confused on this major point. It's the reason there are so many unhappy and indifferent people in the employment marketplace: They have sold their soul for a mess of potage. Told ten years ago of a growing need for linguists, the unemployed Ph.D. linguist is a bitter man today— there are few jobs in this field. Did someone tell you about the shortage of librarians five years ago? The country is wallowing in library science majors today. Space engineering is the wave of the future? Tell that to the guy pumping gas in San Jose—ask to see his degrees.

The laws of supply and demand are as applicable in the marketplace as in the commodity market; a boom market for soybeans today means a bear market tomorrow. "Desperate Need for Computer Programmers" screams a headline in the trade press five years ago; today they are battling for occupational survival. But that's true in any field.

Job seekers should identify what it is they *want* to do and forget about the oversupply of talent; those who do what they love are going to be much more effective than those who labor out of obligation or a misplaced emphasis on security. Three out of four college graduates will quit their first entrance-level professional job within two years of graduation. Because they did what they "should" and not what they wanted.

"Well, gee, I've 'wanted' plenty of jobs and never gotten them."

Now you're putting me on.

There's an enormous difference between the dream and the reality. Your ability to "function" as a cost accountant, airline sales rep, or economic negotiator is of prime importance.

Most job seekers are fundamentally disparate: What they want, they can't do; what they do, they don't want. That's why there are so many indifferent teachers, salesmen, soldiers, bureaucrats, and managers in our society. They are not in touch or can't seem to get in touch with their real feelings. And if they discover what it is they *want* to do, the anxiety caused by this self-knowledge immobilizes them. That's why the smart employer will delve into the real wants of his best candidate and make the hard judgment of whether his flair and job objective are complementary.

"Knowing what we want terrifies us?"

Paralyzes.

The reasons are not difficult to discover. From infancy through adolescence into senility, we are *trained* to want what *others* want. Parents, educators, the clergy, the military, and all employers have a hand in making people "duty-bound" to some organization's objectives.

To divest oneself of this hair-shirted straitjacket is a full-time job. And it terrifies people to turn away from their education and experience, which fit them to fulfill objectives they usually don't want for themselves. Accordingly, employers need to probe to find out if the job candidate sitting before him wants his job or simply feels qualified to fill it. Wanting a job, of course, is not sufficient; being qualified is not enough. But being *willing* and *able* is the ticket of admission to buying into a job, on the one hand, and personal motivation on the job, on the other.

So if you are in the business of hiring people, then it is in your interests to find out what people *want* and why they want it. The more candor from your candidates the better, because the only "secret" about matching up the right man or woman for *the* job is giving the employment nod to that person who *wants* the job and can do it.

Only about one of ten candidates for any judgment job will make the grade.

"How do you spot willing and able people for growth jobs?"

If you have a flair at matchmaking, it's purely unscientific and strictly hunch. The best matchmakers scorn pre-employment tests, psychological profiles, and discount the educational/experiential factor.

Effective employers zero-in on the flair factor. In addition, they want answers to the following questions:

1. Which candidates' eyes lit up when the job was discussed? (Personnel administrators will blanch at the thought, but the eyes of a job candidate reveal far more than a résumé.)

2. Did the job candidate call back frequently? Is he eager?

3. If the job candidate has the talent, the flair, to do the job, what significant achievements in the candidate's background prove he has this talent?

4. Will he take risks? What proof does he offer?

5. Find out *why* he *wants* your job. Is your job a mission or a meal-ticket?

6. Is he a mugwump? That is, is he independent, self-reliant? Can you count on him to agree and disagree with *conviction?*

7. Do the candidate's job objectives match your organizational objectives?

8. Did he seem in touch with his own feelings, or did he try to *please* you?

9. Most important, what *challenges* your best candidate about your job? How will your job test him?

10. Is he honest?

Next an employer confronts his own hidden agenda.

"What do you mean by the expression 'hidden agenda'?"

The unconscious's power over our routine thinking processes. A potent force, indeed, and *the major factor* in why we decide on hiring *this* woman and not *that* man. Saying *you* are free from these unconscious considerations in the employment process is going to land you in Big Trouble, if it already hasn't done so. Maybe that's why you're reading this book!

"I have a gut reaction, Mac, about this guy: I think he fits my goals; my viscera say he's right for our programming job."

Whenever you hear something like that from a person in your firm (and I hear the equivalent every working day of my life), it means that hunch and instinct, the hidden motivators buried deep within the old id, have made their mark. Somebody is about to be hired (or fired) or promoted or switched on the job because a hidden agenda is satisfied.

"But you said acting on one's hunches is smart."

It's also madness. My point is to make you discover the *method* in your madness.

Acting on *hunch* is right. Not understanding what your hunch, your hidden agendas are, is crazy. Hunch decisions can work against you. Are you hiring this person because you want someone

- lousy so you'll look good?
- who takes orders and buttons his lip?
- who is loyal, obedient, and trustworthy?
- your boss would like?
- as a lunch companion?

There are as many reasons as there are employers and job candidates. Never solely trust your own judgment. Subject every candidate to a bevy of interviews elsewhere in your division or firm. This strategy screens out and surfaces your hidden agendas and makes you look at them with clinical objectivity.

The only question, remember, you want answered is, "Is this person effective?"

Stick to the flair factor.

"But I've always been told to focus on a candidate's job history."

That's what Abe Lincoln did.

The very best men and women in our society are changing jobs (and, less frequently, "careers") with an ease that would have discomfited our Calvinist forebears. Most good people have three or four "careers" during an occupational lifetime and a score of employers. To dwell, as an employer, too much on the "stability" factor (*"Why,* this person has had five jobs in the past seven years!") is to be out of step with the times and out of tune with the people who can do your organization a good turn.

Good people, like good organizations, are constantly changing. In the process of change, growth often occurs: I am not the person I was in 1967, nor are you, and neither are any of the organizations we worked for then (even if we are still employed at the same place). Accordingly, savvy employers will take into account that change is the only invariable law of life, that people are changing all the time, and that it's the employer's supreme responsibility to judge whether a candidate is changing into something *his* organization can use.

"From what you're saying, people must be alert, otherwise the good job they hold today will be gone tomorrow."

You'd better believe it.

Organizational good health implies a continual "in, up, and out" work atmosphere. If the best people in our society are changing jobs (even if within the *same* organization) vastly more than their parents did, then employers must be quick-footed to hire a job candidate at the apex of his occupational curve and discharge him at his nadir.

It's easy to say.

Like averring that the best time to buy stocks is when the market is low, and the best time to sell is when the market is dear.

But from an organization's point of view, occupational circulation among the people who make the place *work* prevents organizational arteriosclerosis, tones up an institution's objectives, and keeps it alive. No matter what the institution, its history usually involves managers "losing touch"—not being in tune with the market, a particular constituency, or new needs and pressures within society. A turnover in the best jobs within your organization assures a fresh perspective—not necessarily the right one, mind you—but new angles of vision. And that's why those you hire for judgment jobs should move up smartly within your organization or leave pronto. That's why every manager needs training in the fine art of churning his "personnel account" (that is, jobs under his domain) so as to stay at least even with the rapidly changing times.

You must learn how to hire people. But before doing that, you need to learn how to fire them. How can you hire Mr. or Ms. Right if you haven't cleared the blank ammunition from the organizational deck of the division you head? How, in a word, are you going to fill a slot with the best available person if the job is still occupied by a man or woman you can't bear to confront and show the door?

"So you can't hire until you learn how to fire?"

The art of firing key people is an essential to any manager's development. A favorite question headhunters query of anxious executives sniffing out new jobs is, "By the way, how many people in the course of your work have you fired . . . and how?" A good rule is never to hire a manager who hasn't learned to fire people. This lack in his supervisory makeup could be a built-in booby trap and blow up in the face of whoever hired him. Remember, hiring and firing *are the central responsibilities of management*. Organizations that abandon this principle are managed thenceforth by executive committees, collectivized soviets, or by appeals to "personnel manuals"—all of which signal organizations in inevitable decline.

"If people are trained to find jobs and continually move from position to position, how do you expect anyone ever to become expert at anything?"

Ticket punchers.

Moving in and out of jobs and organizations with the sinuosity a snake would envy.

Different from job jumpers, who always move up in terms of responsibility or quality of job (even though they might necessarily move *down* in pay), ticket punchers are main-chance operators. Ambitious for the quick score, ticket punchers are to the world of work what social climbers are to the universe of society.

Ticket punchers are easily spotted. Name-dropping, glibness, bluff, and shallow charm make them marked for life. Eschew at all cost.

Of course ticket punchers are not expert at anything: Never long enough at a job to learn, their only chance at occupational survival is to glide so quickly across the surface of the pond that nobody knows whether they made a ripple.

Close inspection of work history, a few well-placed phone calls to employers, and the repeated question, "What, in fact, did you do at ABC, Inc.?" quickly discourage the chronic ticket punchers.

"Isn't there some easier way to hire and fire people?"

The head shrinkers are into a lot of good stuff. Maybe in fifty years we can hire managers the same way we qualify aviators.

But for the time being, all we have to go on is the suspicion that whatever our personal flair factors, whatever our achievement orientation, our accomplishment index—call it what you will—that this *talent* might very well be a product of the unconscious mind.

What do I mean?

Well, don't rip this book into little pieces and stuff into the garbage disposal, but my hunch—after ten years in the business—is that the unconscious, where neuroses are alive and well, plays a misunderstood role in underpinning our *talent* or flair on a job.

The water is a trifle deep at this point, and at the risk of pulling us both down past our depth, let me just say that I believe it could be that:

- headhunters suffer from an acute case of "the disease to please."
- police officers harbor a secret criminal urge.
- firemen are latent pyromaniacs.
- correction officers live vicariously through their probationers.
- crisis managers are paranoiacs.
- academics are frustrated underachievers.
- engineers suffer from decision phobia.

All of this is probably balderdash. My point, joking aside, is that nowhere near enough study has been done by the shrinks, industrial engineers, and clinical psychologists in this area of employment preference and effectiveness. People who want to program themselves for success (this is my only point on the subject) need to look under the covers at psychic phenomena of which they are consciously unaware. What you might find will not please, but it could certainly inform.

CHAPTER 5

Résumés and the résuméd

"What questions should an employer ask himself before beginning his candidate search?"

Some of the questions I ask myself (or a client) follow:

1. Why can't this task be eliminated or its duties combined with another job filled by someone who is able, deserving, and willing within the organization? No? Are you sure? Think again.

2. What is the point of the task, its *objective?* If it lay vacant "would the heavens fall," as Uncle Sam Ervin is wont to say? If your answer is a weak "No," go back to question No. 1. Who else's approval is necessary? Who, as a courtesy, should concur?

3. Does the hiring authority have the clout to negotiate salary? If not, who does?

4. What is the salary range?

5. What are the flair factors?

6. How much time do you have to fill the job?

7. How many candidates should you interview?

8. What is the "accomplishment" factor in the task? What challenge will turn the right person on?

9. Who does the task now?

10. What about overlap?

11. Does the task deal primarily with people, data, money, things, or ideas?

12. What happens when the task is done?

13. Do you have résumés on potential candidates?

"Résumés? I thought most organizations require application forms."

To inflict an application form on every yahoo who passes through your doors or seeks employment via the mails is cruel and unusual punishment designed by personnel functionaries to discourage people from finding gainful employment. Application forms, like the IRS's Form 1040, killeth the human spirit. And plenty of organizations actually code and file (!) these completed forms "for future reference." It boggles the mind, but most low-level administrative types would rather murder their children than destroy an official form of the organization. The world will end in neither a bang nor a whimper; the last sound you hear is the hum of the Xerox machine.

"Where do people apply for a job in your ideal organization?"

Not in the personnel department, which unless they want a job in personnel, is the last place people will find a job they want.

Far better to eliminate the personnel department. Let each department do its own hiring. The paperwork, as little as possible, should be done in your finance, accounting, or controller section.

Don't saddle your organization with any more paper requirements than absolutely necessary. Routinely chuck all résumés six months old and older.

"If finance absorbs the personnel department, what do you do with the other personnel functions?"

Which are paper problems, right?

Put the paperwork about people—the so-called personnel action papers—in finance.

Separating the personnel function from finance is dumb. Because people are a *direct* expense. Direct costs of peoples' salaries far exceed plant overhead, supplies, and travel costs.

Repeatedly, in my experience in business, government, and the vast gray area of institutions in between, when the going is rough, it's because of a money snarl.

A project director fails to clear a raise for a key person with finance.

A job slot created for the new whiz kid in programming isn't blessed by the comptroller.

The salary of a new vice president the boss wants to use in his West Coast operation queers up next year's fiscal planning.

All solvable problems.

If people sit down and thrash out the dollar-and-cent realities.

Making your finance man the "personnel" manager eliminates another unnecessary step in making manpower decisions.

Moreover, if your organization must systematize leave records, attendance reports, transfers—"personnel actions"—then finance, which has a computer accounting capacity (what are personnel "processes" but accounting responsibilities?), is the place that has the action.

"What about hiring support personnel—certainly there should be a department to do that?"

You mean secretaries, clerks, stock boys, factotums, right?

Well, in my judgment secretarial jobs are vitally important and the hiring for these crucial jobs should be done on a department-wide, not company-wide, basis. But if you don't do things that way where you work, certainly staff services or whatever you call it is the place to do the hiring.

Eliminating (which is to say, dispersing) the "personnel" function is another device Top Management should use to decentralize and individualize corporate behavior. Personnel people might fight this action. But if your organization adopts my simple plan, "personnel" work is going to be a lot more fun and productive than the current structure allows.

"Throw away the application form! What about résumés?"

There are only two important questions the résumé answers: (1) Do you want to interview its author? (2) Does the author know who he is, what he wants, and what he can do?

Nobody in his or her right mind ever hired a résumé. No matter how good.

Résumés are promotional literature, advertisements for oneself. The fact that most résumés are horrendously ineffective only bears out the poor opinion job seekers have of themselves.

So in plowing through a hundred résumés on your desk, ask yourself these questions:

How well put together is the candidate under scrutiny? What does he want? What can he do? What proof does he have of both?

And second, on the basis of the piece of paper before you, is it really worth your time (you cost out, remember, at thirty dollars an hour) to see the man or woman under inspection?

People who study résumés, insist on seeing them before interviewing good candidates who don't happen to have them, or as with the U. S. Civil Service's Form 171 (Application for Employment), actually assign "points" for each "hard" piece of information contained therein, are anathema to headhunters, people persons, and organizational leaders trying to make people down the line hire the best people available.

That's why, I bet, half the people reading this book would agree that the good jobs they found required neither an application form nor a résumé. Most people find jobs through the hidden job network, a colleague of a friend whose boss's special assistant is looking for a good man or woman to be deputy director of the firm's transportation component.

"Are you saying résumés are a waste of time?"

Certainly not for the people who write them!

Job seekers with first-rate résumés simply generate far more interviews than those who have poor or mediocre background summaries.

For employers, however, knowing how to screen and *read* résumés is very important, if you want to consider as many people as possible for a position. And screening résumés means being ruthless with those pieces of paper which don't communicate anything except a few dry facts—throw out these résumés, pronto.

"Why do employers interview people using résumés?"

Because they are unaccustomed to the interviewing process, feel insecure (often more uncomfortable than the job candidates themselves), and like to hide behind a piece of paper, letting it, the résumé, guide the interview.

But the whole point of a résumé is to gain an interview. Once that's accomplished, once the living, breathing item is staring you right in the face, to hide behind a piece of paper and affect to find *there* more than what is sitting in your deep-set, leather, brown couch not ten feet away, is a confession of insecurity hardly becoming the "hiring authority."

Demanding résumés also postpones interviews. Overworked employers thus straight-arm job applicants by insisting on the piece of paper before interviews. Which is O.K. if you have time to wait.

"But don't most employers study a résumé and compare it with others?"

Some do. But I can't figure out what they "compare."

Most employers hardly look at a résumé once an interview begins. And most smart hiring people *never* require it if they trust the judgment of a person recommending the job candidate. Moreover, most résumés are so bad that plenty of normally potent effectives in the executive work force *can't* find a job via the résumé route.

I must have seen well over twenty thousand résumés in the past ten years.

A few résumés stand out as examples of how to be "sold" on someone you've never seen. Most résumés, however, are so like one another that it's impossible to make an educated judgment.

What it costs is an hour of your time. So if you must wade through a hundred résumés, before you establish your interview schedule, pick out those pieces of paper that reflect some competence on the author's part. If anyone cares so little about himself, is so shy of revealing who he really is, is so modest about his occupational triumphs and achievements that he can't or won't give you a clue in his résumé, the chances are good that he can't put your organization first. This same lack of self-esteem—so vital in functioning not only on the job but off—will carry over on the job and will diminish your organization accordingly.

"Don't good résumés conceal far more than they reveal?"

Sometimes.

Especially when they are prepared by someone *other* than the job candidate.

Not good employment strategy.

Now, of course, there are good résumés . . . and outstanding résumés. And one of the most disappointing experiences a hiring-type can live through is to turn onto someone on paper and know five minutes into the interview that the advertising doesn't fit the product. This is probably because a professional résumé-writing service is talking to you rather than the human being sitting in front of you. Or a career advisory service has put its mark on the man or woman in front of you.

The best career counselors make their clients do the work. They don't write résumés, generate interviews, or bird-dog jobs. That's each job seeker's responsibility.

"What's the first thing to look for on a résumé?"

Job goals.

The trouble with most people looking for a job is not knowing what they *want*. They look for "what's available." No wonder they can't find a good job!

So, in reviewing résumés, zero-in on the candidate's job objectives before anything else. Who cares if he went to Groton, West Point, and Harvard Law if what he wants isn't what you need? Or is listed in Who's Who in American Colleges and Universities in 1954 (at least half of the candidates I interview report such a crucial fact; to this day, I don't want to know what *this means*). Pound-for-pound, square-inch-for-square-inch—there is more trivia in résumés than the Congressional Record.

O.K.

Of fifty résumés on your desk, maybe (an optimistic "maybe"), four people *want* what you have. And if your job fits half of his wants, then that qualifies him.

Now you want a quick summary of the man/woman.

In the nineteenth century, authors synopsized every chapter with a lead paragraph in italics about what was going to happen to Long John Silver in Chapter Six. Smart job seekers sum up where they've been, who they are, and—in capsule form—what they can *do*. This paragraph should grab you by the nape of the neck and *order* you to reach out, pick up the phone, and call him in Calgary. More often, it tells you whether you want to read on into the body of the résumé. Like a good book jacket, a summary of background persuades you to browse farther into the text. Employers can usually tell whether there is a symmetrical conformity between what a person wants (his job objectives), who a person *is*, and what he *does* from this preliminary paragraph.

Job seekers are wont, of course, to misrepresent themselves at this point. The romantic imagination supersedes the realistic approach. A candidate's fancy, so beautifully expressed in his job objectives, is not supported by what follows in the résumé. The triumph of aspiration over achievement. The fanciful muse out of touch with terra firma. Such candidates, to their credit, at least *have* an imagination. Goals, no matter how unreal. Which, as we have seen, is untrue of most people on the job market.

"How should a résumé help an employer? Doesn't a job candidate retail his list of jobs, last to first?"

That's the trouble. Unless there is direct evidence that each job led upward in the same field in terms of money and responsibility, there is nowhere near enough information about what the job candidate does well.

I like job seekers to break down their background functionally. What talent do they market? And does this flair support the job or jobs the candidate wants?

"What kind of flair factors do you look for in a person's résumé?"

That's an unanswerable question unless you take into account the kind of job you are trying to fill. Certainly the flair factor or talent I would search out on paper for a political organizer, say, would be entirely different than if I wanted to hire an industrial engineer.

Let's say as an employer, you need to find someone with demonstrated mediation, persuasion, and conciliation skills. O.K. Of the résumés on your desk, how many job seekers actually relate under the appropriate heading this talent (e.g. contracting capability, middleman experience, broker skills—the euphemisms are endless). Clearly, if the candidate makes an impressive case on paper, he is worth interviewing. And at this point, that's the only decision you need to make: whether someone, on the basis of a piece of paper, is worth looking over.

Each heading captions four or five actual "achievements" of the job candidate—four or five examples, *par excellence,* of his analytical ability, management expertise, project leadership, etc.

All of this information gives me some idea whether this person is really worth taking the time to interview.

"Is there anything else you look for in a résumé?"

After reading about a job candidate's real skills, I'll review his "personal data" section—education, age, sex, marital status, salary requirements, health limitations, et al. If mine is a traveling job and the candidate won't, then into the round file with the résumé. Need someone who can jog four miles without breathing hard? And your candidate has chronic bronchitis. Out it goes.

Finally, I like references included. What is their caliber? Are they easily reached by phone?

Let's look at an example of first-rate functional résumés. And let's assume that our job is to find a deputy public relations man or woman for a professional athletic team on the Eastern Seaboard.

Mortimer Rizenoff
3205 Eudore Boulevard
Mountain View, Maryland 20777
Telephone: (301) 778-8663
Age: 23   Single

VOCATIONAL OBJECTIVE

Seek responsible position in athletic- or recreation-oriented organization, especially in public/community relations, front-office management, or administrative role. Particularly qualified in communications (promotions, press relations, advertising) and organization (traveling secretary, scheduling, recreational programs). Desire to use strong sports orientation in conjunction with such demonstrated abilities as marketing, public speaking. Welcome high pressure, long hours. Willing to travel and/or relocate.

SUMMARY OF BACKGROUND

B.A. and M.A. in international relations. President of student government and advertising editor of yearbook in high school. Interests and activities, including volunteer work, focusing on sports. Extensive background in black culture and history, and crosscultural communications. Worked in community for telephone company during summers. Despite my specialized background, my education and outside activities have developed flexibility and skills applicable to fulfilling most requirements of a sports-related position.

SKILLS AND INTERESTS OF POTENTIAL VALUE

Active participant and informed, compulsive spectator of all sports. Accepted as member of sports-oriented fraternity, Phi Gamma Delta, although not a varsity athlete; active participant and organizer of interfraternity league teams. Organized and supervised a "Sports Club" for fourth-, fifth-, and sixth-grade boys on volunteer basis; developed educational programs and activities relating to their interests. As volunteer, helped co-ordinate and conduct recreational activities during summers at church Bible school; also bike hikes for elementary school students. Have always given the highest priority to sports activities, enabling me to devote myself full-time to a vocation in this field.

COMMUNICATION SKILLS

Addressed assemblies of up to 2,500 people in both prepared and extemporaneous situations. Conducted meetings for wide spectrum of groups, including both parents and students, at local, county, and state levels. Interaction with other student government groups in seminars, meetings, student exchanges. Direct relationship with business community in soliciting and developing advertisments for yearbook. Effective crosscultural communication in Europe; while proficient in French, was also able to communicate effectively with people of German, Italian, and Spanish origins. Able to communicate confidently with both large groups and individuals in both business and informal situations.

LEADERSHIP AND ORGANIZATIONAL SKILLS

Elected and appointed to many positions throughout school, such as president and financial secretary of student government. Organized and co-ordinated schoolwide candy sale grossing approximately $10,000. Initiated and supervised new orientation format in high school; served on Orientation Committee at Hopkins. Elected council chairman at Maryland Association of Student Councils Workshop. Chosen as school representative to statewide American History Conference; sole Hopkins representative to nationwide Naval Academy Foreign Affairs Conference, 1970. As advertising editor, developed national award-winning ad campaign for yearbook, including soliciting, planning, designing, billing, and collecting for ads. Co-ordinated student housing program for Johns Hopkins summer program in Geneva on extremely limited budget. These activities have taught me to be effective both as a leader-organizer and as a participant in varied projects at all levels.

SPECIAL ABILITIES

Work well under intense pressure. Able to meet specific deadlines and work long hours if needed. Met every deadline for yearbook, some with extended hours. Do well in timed examinations.

Able to work with details. In physical sense, built own stereo receiver and carved wooden ship model; drawing ability. Otherwise, able to remember and deal with minute details in organizing and executing projects, such as co-ordinating travel in Europe, both individually and in groups.

Able to work with figures. Financial accounting in student government, church, and personal accounts. Scored 770/800 in SAT math, 34/35 in FSEE quantitative reasoning. Highest grades in class in advanced math, probability, and statistics in graduate school. Designed own scoreboards and kept score of every All-Star baseball game during childhood, and every other game attended.

EDUCATION

Accepted for five-year B.A.-M.A. program at The Johns Hopkins University, leading to M.A. from School of Advanced International Studies in 1973. Included summer of 1970 of study and independent travel in Europe. Full fellowship at SAIS; B.A.-M.A. and Maryland Senatorial Scholarships at Hopkins. Many scholastic awards, including National Honor Society (1966) and National Merit Scholarship letter of commendation (1967).

PERSONAL DATA

Born August 9, 1951; single; excellent health, 5'10", 145 lbs.

WORK EXPERIENCE

Summers of 1968, 1969, and 1971, worked for telephone company as frameman and installer-repairman.

Volunteer work at Bladensburg Elementary School as organizer-leader of "Sports Club," 1972.

Part-time work selling art supplies at Woodward and Lothrop, winter of 1972–73.

A great résumé; all it lacks is a summary of actual employment and—a serious lapse—a list of references.

"Why would you want to interview this fellow?"

Well, for openers:

1. This is a PR job and of 150 résumés on my desk; but only five are adequate public-relations material! Since this candidate can market himself, the chances are good that he will do a fine job for my client.

2. This fellow looks inexpensive—twenty-three years old! The chances are good that he won't want $25,000 per annum. Money isn't the most important thing to an employer; only the second most important.

3. Mortimer knows what he wants. His vocational objective fits 100 per cent that quintessential summary my client couldn't write about his job!

4. The résumé, while clearly promotional, isn't slick—no acetate cover, no cutesy photographs and mindless blurb seen so often in the résumés of people into public relations.

5. The guy is clearly a compulsive sports freak—my client loves to play baseball trivia, like who played shortstop for the Philadelphia Phillies in 1956 (Granny Hamner?). I'll find this out in the interview.

There's plenty more in this résumé. But the point is that *I want* to interview him. And if this fellow's paper doesn't match the product, if there is more embroidery here than whole cloth, I'll know that in ten minutes and show him the door.

Of the 150 résumés I rifled through to pick five candidates to interview, this and four others stood out. After interviewing all five, comparative profiles are easy. Of the five, one is going to stand out clearly as the man or woman for the job. The point is that the interviews, not the résumés you reviewed, finally make up your mind.

So what, if probably twenty people with inadequate résumés are better for the job than the five you picked! At an hour an interview, that's 150 hours, or nearly four work weeks! And you at thirty dollars per hour—that's forty-five hundred dollars. Not exactly a cost-beneficial use of your time!

"I'm confused. Are you saying managers should rely either on résumés or the hidden manpower pool?"

Neither. Shrewd employers will use *any* source of willing and able candidates. Employers who restrict themselves to the hidden manpower pool or to résumés received over the transom or using want ads or specialized headhunting firms nix themselves. Cast a wide net to find the right person for your tough job. And that goes for cold-turkey job applicants who drop in unannounced. Even if you are too busy to see them, detail this job to a bright assistant. Chances are good someone with the gumption to show up and ask for a job is just the person you're looking for to untangle that messy problem you have in East Cleveland.

"Did this guy land the job?"

As an assistant PR director with a major league team and a flag contender.

The ironic factor is that Mortimer, at age twenty-three, was never professionally employed in his life, much less with any formal experience in public relations. Note in his résumé how artfully he conceals (without omitting entirely) his strong economics/international relations orientation.

Why?

Because it didn't support the job he wanted.

This résumé is an excellent example of a person who zeroed in on his accomplishments, none of which were particularly experiential or academic, and included the kind of information that really supported a job he *wanted*.

Remember, really *wanting* a job is an important qualification.

"Any more examples?"

Well, since you asked . . .

Let's suppose our *Fortune* 500 firm is looking to establish its own in-house management service component. Our CEO is tired of paying a 250 per cent overhead and fee to outsiders. The top two people for this unit have been chosen, and they need to recruit from within or without the company a middle-level staff ranging from fifteen thousand dollars to twenty-five thousand dollars in salary. Our business is computerized information systems, software specialists for industry.

Which of the following two résumés is persuasive?

Richard Mills
60 Longfellow Street, Apt. 18-H
Cambridge, Massachusetts 02142
(617) 490-8298

PERSONAL DATA

Age: 28
Married, no children
U.S. citizen

OBJECTIVE

Management consulting, with emphasis in areas of strategic and financial planning, and management decision-support systems. Ideal position will be in a consulting firm with opportunities for increasing responsibility and continuing professional growth; or alternatively, as an internal consultant in a firm where the potential exists to build or manage an internal service group.

STRENGTHS

Solid background and nine years of experience in multiple sides of a growing technology-based business.
  • marketing and financial planning
  • sales support
  • engineering and product planning and development.
Sensitivity to the requirements of working on a day-to-day basis with clients and client organizations, developed through sales support and consulting experience.

Well-practiced spoken and written communication skills, ranging from presentations to customers and management, to technical report writing and preparation of user communication.

Project supervision experience directing the activities of from one to five people.

Well-developed analytical and administrative skills, building upon technical undergraduate and business administration graduate degrees.

Extensive practical experience and research in the analysis, design, and implementation of management information and decision-support systems.

EDUCATION

(1972–74) SLOAN SCHOOL OF MANAGEMENT, MASSACHUSETTS INSTITUTE OF TECHNOLOGY (Cambridge, Massachusetts)

Candidate for Master of Science in management degree in June 1974. Concentration in managerial planning and control, with related courses in organization studies, finance, and information systems. Thesis describes organizational and situational factors in the successful implementation of management decision-support systems. Summer research assistant in corporate strategy and planning project. Teaching assistant in managerial accounting course.

(1970–72) ARIZONA STATE UNIVERSITY (Tempe, Arizona)

Bachelor of Science degree in mathematics, *summa cum laude*. Completed undergraduate work at night while working full-time.

(1963–65) DARTMOUTH COLLEGE (Hanover, New Hampshire)

Majored in mathematics. Research assistant for Dartmouth Time-Sharing Project. Received Alfred P. Sloan Scholarship Award.

PROFESSIONAL EXPERIENCE

(1972–74) HONEYWELL INFORMATION SYSTEMS, INC. (Wellesley, Massachusetts)

Part-time consultant to manager of Business Plan Evaluation. Designed and implemented interactive computer model to support systematic evaluation by marketing and planning management of alternative product line and marketing strategies.

(1970–72) HONEYWELL INFORMATION SYSTEMS, INC. (Phoenix, Arizona)

Member of headquarters marketing staff for Honeywell's 6000 line of large computer systems. Recommended market strategies (product evolution, pricing). Developed five-year sales forecasts and financial evaluations to support alternative plans.

Wrote product plans for hardware and operating system products. Collaborated with engineers, salesmen, market researchers, and factory cost analysts to integrate their requirements into these plans. Presented technical seminars for management and customers. Cochairman of software design review board.

(1969–70) GENERAL ELECTRIC COMPANY, INFORMATION SYSTEMS EQUIPMENT DIVISION (Phoenix, Arizona)

Software planning specialist in division planning group. Activities and responsibilities similar to those with Honeywell (above), for operating system and application program software on GE–600 product line.

Special assignment as project leader for systems engineering product development team (five people).

(1969) GENERAL ELECTRIC COMPANY, INFORMATION SYSTEMS EQUIPMENT DIVISION (Bethesda, Maryland)

Directed all onsite and field technical support for test market of a GE new-business venture, the RESOURCE service bureau system. Trained salesmen and assisted customers in use of system. Installed and maintained system software. Assisted operations staff with development of procedure and performance measurement systems.

Extensively interviewed customers as part of test market analysis. Recommended product and strategy changes. Assisted management with organization planning and recruiting for permanent organization.

(1968–69) GENERAL ELECTRIC COMPANY, AIRCRAFT ENGINE GROUP (Lynn, Massachusetts)

Member of computer center technical staff. Evaluated computer equipment proposals (factory data collection system, microfiche applications). Prepared project plans and budgets. Developed procedures for scheduling, measurement, and analysis of computer operations. Consulted to application programmers in programming techniques and system use. Maintained operating system software for two large computer systems.

Division representative to GE Corporate Task Force on Operating Systems. Wrote and presented major portion of final report to management.

(1965–68) GENERAL ELECTRIC COMPANY, INFORMATION SYSTEMS MARKETING (Wakefield, Massachusetts)

Applications engineer in New England District. Prepared technical proposals and made presentations to prospects to support sales of GE computer systems. Designed data communications applications with customer personnel. Prepared and taught customer training classes. Project leader for major GE-635 system installation. Directed efforts of other application engineers in conversion of application programs, field test and maintenance of system software, and acceptance testing. Responsible to account manager for all technical support to customer.

A good résumé. But it could be better. There is no summary of background, but there is an excellent summary of work experience (a trifle long, perhaps) and, again, no references are included. Now let's look at the kind of résumés we see most every day.

Hays Worthington
4438 Graham Road
Lake Serenity, Idaho
(208) 673-4218

JOB GOALS:

To seek a line management position in a profit-making firm.

PERSONAL:
Birthdate: August 16, 1946
Birthplace: Salt Lake City, Utah
Marital Status: Single

EDUCATION:
Georgetown University School of Foreign Service
Honors: *Summa cum laude*
Activities: President, Young Democrats

EXPERIENCE: (November 1972 to present)
Information Systems data processor
Michael-Wells, Inc.
McLean, Virginia

(May to August 1971)
Microdata coding clerk

Morrison Industries
Purchase, North Dakota

References and writing samples on request.

Which would you interview first?

"What kind of résumés do employers generally receive?"

The résumé *form* is generally the same—descriptive, chronological, or what I call an "obit" résumé, as if the candidate were six feet under. The content of the résumé, of course, varies from one industry to another. Let's take law, for example. I'm not a lawyer and never hired one for anything but nonlegal employment, but let's look at three standard résumés of young men anxious to break into law practice.

MICHAEL C. CRAMER
1812 Connecticut Avenue, N.W.
Washington, D.C. 20036
(202) 333-4156

Preferred Fields of Practice: Patent, Corporate, or General Law Practice

EDUCATION:

Legal: Georgetown University Law Center, Washington, D.C. (1970–present)
Candidate for Juris Doctor, May 1974
Academic: 56 credit hours
  EXCEPTIONAL: Constitutional Law
  DISTINGUISHED: Commercial Paper, Tax I, Business Associations, Evidence, and Administrative Law.
  GOOD: Decedents' Estates, Tax II, Corporations, Property, Environmental Law, Criminal Justice I and II, Contracts, Torts, and Civil Procedure
  PASS: None
Course: As required, with electives in Corporate and Patent Law.

College: New York University Washington Square College, New York, New York
B.A. *cum laude,* 1970

Major: History
Honors: Dean's list
          Freshman of the Year
          Honors in History

Preparatory: Catonsville Senior High School, Baltimore, Maryland
Graduated 1966, approximately thirteenth in class of 345.

EMPLOYMENT EXPERIENCE:

(1972–73) Law Clerk, Civil Division, Justice Department, Washington, D.C.
(part-time employment) Duties included: Review and summarization of statute revisions to be distributed to U.S. attorneys, extensive research, the writing of memoranda, pleadings, and letters in response to inquiries from private citizens.

(Summer 1973) Law Clerk—Myers, Moore and McIntosh, Washington, D.C.
(summer employment) Duties included extensive research, complete brief writing, investigation, and preparation of cases for trial.

NONLEGAL EXPERIENCE

Claims Clerk, Veterans Administration, Washington, D.C.
Evaluated claims for educational assistance to determine eligibility.
United States Army, two years' active duty and honorably discharged, June 1966. Rifleman and squad leader.

PERSONAL

Born: July 13, 1945, Baltimore, Maryland; married with no children.

PHILLIP J. MARKOWSKI
1335 North Van Dorn
Alexandria, Virginia 22203
(703) 345-2378

PERSONAL:

Birthdate: May 2, 1947
Birthplace: Boise, Idaho
Marital Status: Married

EDUCATION:

Legal: University of Virginia School of Law—J.D., 1973
Charlottesville, Virginia

Honors: Graduated No. 2 in class of 135
Activities: Environmental Law Society Member, Phi Alpha Delta legal
            fraternity Participant, Moot Court competition
College: University of Nebraska—B.A., 1969
Lincoln, Nebraska
  Major: Political science
  Honors: Nebraska state scholarship, 1966–69
  Activities: President, Young Republicans
              Student Association President, 1968

EXPERIENCE:

Legal Assistant
(November 1972–present) Office of Civil Compliance, Law Enforcement Assistance Administration U. S. Department of Justice, Washington, D.C.
Special Assistant
(May–August 1971) Congressman Charles Thone, House of Representatives, Washington, D.C.
Law Clerk
(June–August 1970) United States Attorney's Office, Boise, Idaho
Law Clerk
(May–June 1970) Meyers, McCluskey, Powers & Tufts, Boise, Idaho
(1966–69) Summer and part-time employment includes tugboat assistant, forklift operator, bartender, bank teller, and tree surgeon.

REFERENCES AND WRITING SAMPLES:
Will be forwarded on request.

PETER J. BROWNSTEIN
Local Address:
355 East Capitol Street
Washington, D.C. 20003
(202) 445-9007
Permanent Address:
1205 Nunnery Lane
Philadelphia, Pennsylvania 23809
(215) 345-1223
Born: August 13, 1949, Philadelphia, Pennsylvania/Marital status:
Married, no children

EDUCATIONAL BACKGROUND:

Legal—Georgetown University Law Center, Washington, D.C.
J.D. expected, June 1975
Academic: GPA 3.45/4.00 (as of June 1973)
Class Standing: Top 15%
Areas of exceptional scholastic achievement:
  Constitutional Law; Trusts and Estates; Legal Research and
  Writing
Activities: Moot Court competition
        Law Students in Court program, 1972–73
        Staff member, Law Review

College—Harvard University, Cambridge, Massachusetts
A.B. *cum laude* in Economics, June 1972
Honors: Phi Beta Kappa
    Dean's list, four semesters
Activities: Dormitory residence hall manager
        Soccer and basketball intramural teams

Preparatory—Middletown Senior High School, Philadelphia, Pennsylvania
Graduated twenty-third in a class of 45, June 1967

EMPLOYMENT EXPERIENCE:

(Summer 1971) **Law Clerk—Schones & Bradford**, Washington, D.C.
Extensive research and writing in substantive and procedural zoning law; drafted court and agency orders; research and writing on building construction contracts and insurance law.

(Summer 1972) **Law Clerk—Hannibal, Cramer & Marks**, Washington, D.C.
The only clerk for this six-man firm. Duties included extensive research on numerous points of law including the writing of memoranda, briefs, and drafting of writs.

MILITARY EXPERIENCE:

(1967–69) **United States Navy, Officer Candidate School**
Newport, Rhode Island
Commissioned Ensign, Supply Corps, Athens, Georgia
Disbursing officer, supply officer, U.S.S. *Enterprise*
Released from active duty, May 1968, Lieutenant, United States Navy
Reserve, April 1969.

REFERENCES:
Available on request.

"It's hard to tell the difference. How would you read this kind of résumé?"

It's tough, but so long as these men don't want work except as lawyers, the thing to look for are law review experience, relative standing at graduation, and age. It's about all you can tell.

But if you were hiring a legislative aide, this kind of résumé would be hopeless. Ditto for a neighborhood legal services project, for analytical work with a regulatory commission—all jobs where legal knowledge carries the day.

A partner in a law firm is as likely to want to interview the chap who played soccer as for any other reason. That's why obit résumés rarely open doors or cause an interview to happen. It's why most employers, who are busy, dip into the hidden manpower pool for their talent.

"Are there any other uses of a functional résumé?"

Yes, if you are new on the job and inherit a large staff, a smart gimmick is to make everyone who works for you write a functional résumé. First of all, it can be lots of fun. Secondly, it makes people who are leery of the new hired gun focus on himself and share with you what it is that makes Sammy hustle. Thirdly, making people break down their skills functionally suggests new assignments and responsibilities, all of which is excellent fodder for that first interview. Finally, if someone is patently unhappy at his job or not particularly effective, this exercise is a delicate way of making him think about where he should go next!

"Who are the people looking for jobs?"

Two kinds: (1) those who have a job, and (2) those who don't. Now, if you are like most employers, you'll prefer for perverse reasons the former; although if you are prepared to take the time, chances are you'll find better talent (at a lower price) from candidates among the latter.

True, those who have a job (and the security of being able to meet their mortgage payments) reflect a kind of confidence that brings the interview process to a rapid boil without all the shrinking dubiety peculiar to the unemployed, who often reflect the humor of brigands about to walk the plank.

There are four stages most unemployed people go through. Every employer should know these stages well, since a knowledge thereof will give you, the employer, an insight into the psychological frame of mind of your applicants.

"What's the first stage?"

One of the first questions I ask every unemployed person is, "How long has it been since you last worked, and what have you been doing to pass the time?" A helluva lot of sheer bushwa is the result; most job seekers, for some reason, start lying immediately:

"I took a trip to Europe to find myself."
"I've used the last three months for personal growth."
"The wife and I had a second honeymoon," et al.

All are ostensibly true; but my thousands of talks with the unemployed suggest that most have used this first stage between jobs to *avoid* coming to grips with themselves and the future. It is generally a terrible relief for most people to leave the past behind and not face up to the future. It might even be a necessary precondition to finding a good job. The sheer euphoria, relief, and freedom most unemployed feel having the burden of a bad job, a berth in graduate school, or a tedious military assignment lifted from their shoulders condition everyone to this vacation psychology. Most people, particularly under forty, use their unemployment checks to underwrite a little personal "downtime" of their own, prior to facing the facts, which are that man and woman must work to find their identity in this part of the twentieth century.

"What happens when the vacation is over?"

The second stage of the unemployment cycle is marked by unusual, hyperthyroid activity on the job seeker's part. Typically, friends are contacted; résumés are mailed; a good many lunches with well-placed friends ensue. The whole stage is marked by confidence, discovery, checking out the job market. Occasionally, the process pays off—a hidden job with a good friend (or, more likely, a good friend of a good friend). But for the most part, the second stage, which lasts about a month, is another step in avoiding the inevitable question, "What is it that I want to do?"

All the job seeker knows is that *he* needs a job, that unemployment benefits *do* end, that one's children and wife are giving him strange looks on a cold Monday morning.

Psychologically, the job seeker in this stage is in good shape. The whole business of finding a job means renewing old acquaintances, traveling in different occupational mainstreams, trodding new turf. There is lift in his step and a shiny confidence in his manner. Good old Lady Luck will lead him to the right job at the right place for the right amount of money. Dreams of new adventures irradiate this second stage of unemployment.

"Do employers see a lot of unemployed people in this second stage?"

Usually as part of the hidden manpower pool.

But then stage three, the ego erosion phase, begins.

Symptoms: severe depression, hostility, hopelessness, despair. Marked by apathy, incommunicative behavior, rigidity, and family problems. Innocence gives way to irritation, high hopes to black despair, an erect purposefulness to the jobless slouch—a 180-degree shift from Stage 2. This period lasts indefinitely, and some tragic victims of divorce, bankruptcy, and sometimes suicide never pass through it. Depending on the job seeker's survival quotient, this period is prolonged *for as long as he has the means to avoid facing up to his problem.*

Third parties often are called upon to help at this point: career advisory services, psychotherapists, family, and friends. People need help. Most people who fail at anything are on the road to recovery once failure is admitted; angry with themselves, they start accepting as much blame as they project. Many people will accept almost any job in this third stage, but that's bad news for the person and his employer.

"So the fourth stage is when a job seeker is most likely to come to terms with himself and an employer?"

For people determined not to become a statistic in the "hidden" unemployed (those no longer on unemployment insurance and no longer counted, jobless people the Labor Department doesn't want to think about), this fourth and last stage is a period of integration and renewal. The signs are revealed in mature, adult behavior, a stabilization of personality. The grown-up job seeker finally knows what he wants and goes after it.

"What do these four separate stages of unemployment mean to the employer?"

Well, taking them in order, employers had better be mindful of when is the best time to strike up a relationship.

Stage 1:

Usually the best time to negotiate an accord. The newly un- employed have a gift for candor easily lost during the passage of downtime. In the first stage, the job seeker is psychologically in- tact. His ego, cruising for a severe buffeting if two or three months elapse without productive interviews and few job offers, is capable psychologically of going to work without the hum of time's winged chariot in his ears. However, astute employers are mindful that although the prospective jobholder is rested and his self-assurance intact, his self-knowledge index is still low; the first job offer he ac- cepts might be a mistake for employer and employee alike.

So, in hiring those midstream in Stage 1, find out how well your candidate knows himself.

And most importantly, find out whether he wants your job or just a paycheck. People in Stage 1 have not gone through the im- portant lesson-learning experiences the crisis of unemployment offers. Like most other personal trials, unemployment is a gift to change and renewal. The trouble with Stage 1 unemployed is that they neither have the time nor the opportunity to know themselves.

Stage 2:

Employers interviewing Stage 2 types should never hire these nervous nellies. Eager beavers all, the unemployed in this stage need more information about themselves and about jobs before they impress in an interview. Because of a bad dose of the "disease to please," job applicants at this stage show all the wrong cards and don't interview as well as those in Stage 1 or Stage 4. The chances of them making a mistake—that is, accepting any job for the wrong reason (they need one)—is a mistake you, as an em- ployer, will subsidize.

So, at this point in the unemployment cycle, check out how many interviews in his field or functional area the candidate has actually generated, what flair factors support his filling your job opening, and whether more downtime is needed for him to know what he wants and what he can do.

Stage 3:

Not likely to waste your time. At home watching the daytime serials, at the racetrack, or driving the children to ballet lessons, Stage 3 types hate themselves. Most are unable to generate appointments, much less bag a job offer. Attitude characterizes them: wanness of cheek, slouch, dazed eyes, or manic gleams of desperation.

Hard-luck stories, the worst strategy the unemployed use, abound. At this point many unemployed welcome a socialized state, where government *assigns* you a job.

Ruthlessness is the best treatment for the unemployed third stagers. They need to know they are a failure. Supportive counseling, "I'm sure you are going to find a good job," is the last thing people in this stage need.

What they need is a sharp jab in the ribs and some tough talk straight from the shoulder. That's when employment counselors are such a bust. The best counselors for anything—jobs, matrimony, hard drink—are never "nice" people. And that's why so few effective ones are around.

Stage 4:

The last stage is the most propitious part of the cycle. Stage 4 types are graduates of the school of hard knocks, evincing motivation, healthy anxiety, real job objectives: They are now responsible for their own happiness. People into Stage 4 are much better job candidates than the misanthropes, spoiled brats, and nervous nellies from the ranks of the *other* unemployed.

CHAPTER 6

Bird-dogging

"Bird-dogging?"

Headhunting.
Flesh-peddling.
Recruitment.

All names of the same game, which is finding effective people in the strangest places.

Those résumés piled high atop your desk are not necessarily where you will find the right man or woman with those flair factors you need to fill an important job.

That's why you've got to tap into the hidden manpower pool; why you must search out to find effective people—the kind of people who don't read the help-wanted ads, are productive on jobs they already have, and need to be pursued, hustled, and won over to your organization.

Once you have him, grab on and hold tight.

Making the candidate feel hustled—that is, wooed, seduced, and brought to the altar—is the way to win total commitment *before* your superstar is on the payroll. Making someone you want feel wanted, far from spoiling good green fruit, is the quickest way to make your man or woman feel at home and productive. Eschew all this nonsense you learned about familiarity breeding contempt. Establish a warm-blooded relationship *fast,* at the beginning of the pipeline, making transparently clear that you *like* the man or woman you hire.

"How do you recruit in the hidden manpower pool?"

Pressed for time and unable to interview a whole swatch of candidates, most savvy employers call ten associates who traffic in effective people—experts with solid judgment who can recommend first-rate job candidates and/or know where they are available.

That way, since they know who and what you want, smart employers are setting up valid screening mechanisms at hardly any cost in time or money. Moreover, everyone likes to see someone they respect find a good job. Tapping into this hidden manpower pool is the quickest way to solve your recruiting problems. Headhunters make a living doing it. Why can't people who employ, say, three or four people a year do the same?

Finally, actually *recruiting* rather than *hiring* a candidate makes good sense. Remember the importance of wooing, seducing, and bringing good people to the altar. Well, everyone likes to be wanted; your best candidate will become twice as productive on the job (three times faster than normal) if he has no deep deferential inhibitions about why he got the job.

You came to him, right? That showed good judgment on your part, he thinks. And the candidate actually recruited for a job feels a reciprocity and parity with you and your staff far quicker than having come through the front door, all barefoot-boy-with-cheek needing a job.

"Doesn't effective recruitment strategy vary from organization to organization depending on size, purposes, and kinds of jobs offered?"

Right.

Obviously recruiting for a small-bore operation is different from finding the next production chief at G.M. Therefore, no matter where you work some part of this chapter is not going to apply.

"Doesn't recruiting from the hidden manpower pool tend to stereotype the kind of people you interview?"

No university hires its own Ph.D.s.

The Peace Corps doesn't hire just-returned volunteers.

The Ford Foundation should nix its "Princeton connection."

The hidden manpower pool is the easiest source of job candidates to tap. But variety is the key to accurate candidate comparison. So for every candidate you interview from the hidden manpower pool, try picking out an interesting stranger from that stack of résumés on your desk.

Publishers should carefully screen unsolicited manuscripts— vastly more goats than lambs there, to be sure, but hidden talent in our society is the job of leadership—whether in publishing or pharmaceuticals—to discover. The trouble with the hidden man- power pool, the in-house referral network, is that most of your candidates looked "branded." And candidates hired the in-house route suspect the "family connection" got them the job, not native talent. Which creates dependency feelings. And we know now how bad that is, don't we?

"What about using an extensive mailing campaign to tap into this hidden manpower pool?"

Great. If you are throwing a wide net to capture, say, thirty French-speaking agronomists.

But for one-shot judgment jobs, Ma Bell is your best ally.

Recruiting candidates by phone is cheaper and quicker than a clumsy mail campaign. Be sure to maintain accurate log books on in- and outgoing phone calls—when, who, and what you talked about. This way, if three or four people are involved in a search, you keep your wires straight and prevent repeat calls to the *same* people. Nothing is as embarrassing to a good headhunting effort as to approach the same recruitment resource more than once.

"What do you mean by a mailing campaign—writing someone for recommendations on good candidates or directly to candidates them- selves?"

Both.

Need to recruit an epistemologist? Ten to one some mailing house has a list of them. Want to find an epistemologist who speaks French? Ten to one you can use the same list and ask your corre- spondents if they know any francophone philosophers. And so forth.

Most people love to be contacted about helping to fill a job. A far-flung mailing campaign to find the right person for an important job is an excellent public relations tool. It shows your organization cares enough to consult, ask the advice, rely on the counsel of people who, for all I know, might be suppliers or customers of your goods and services. Even if you don't act on all the advice you'll get, people like to be asked. Carried to its extreme, job offers are often made to people certain to turn them down because the organization wants to augment its relationships with a Very Important Person.

"Is the phone blitz an appropriate recruitment tool when you need to find large groups of people?"

It should supplement your mass mailings. And the people you recruit as recruiters are crucial.

Establish a recruitment task force. Make Top Management O.K. the best people you can find, no matter how many managers scream bloody murder after you've raided their department.

"Recruitment task force? Sounds like a big order for my small organization."

Exactly. Swell for large organizations. Not precisely the best policy for organizations who need to fill three or four key jobs a year. Still, whether recruiting for a large conglomerate or a medium-sized business, try picking people who are your best bird-doggers.

"What flair factors do you look for in a recruiter?"

1. An outstanding telephone voice and manner. Someone who sold encyclopedias during his college summer vacation is perfect: telephone tigers. Look for recruiters who will work weekends, which is often the best time to find candidates off guard, relaxed, and thinking about their future.

2. Pick recruiters, where possible, based on their knowledge of the functional skill of person(s) you are trying to recruit. Let space scientists recruit space scientists, editors editors, and so forth.

3. Recruit recruiters who enthuse; it's contagious and superimportant in the headhunting game.

4. Measure results. Reward those who bring back the bearskins.

"Why not let personnel do the recruiting?"

O.K. But how many people in personnel where you work know how the place works? If yours is a large firm or organization, a separate recruitment division might work out. At any rate, recruitment is light-years different from personnel. If you set up a recruitment division, staff it, not with professional recruiters or personnel people, but with functional specialists who have a knack at finding the top people in their trade, craft, field, or career.

"What about headhunters—what do they do, how do they work, and how should you hire them?"

"Executive search specialists," if you're not in the business, or headhunters, if you are, constitute a useful (but by no means the sole) resource in finding hard-to-find people. It's dumb to use headhunters if you can find outstanding people through your own contacts in the hidden manpower pool.

At the same time, some jobs require such unusual flair and are so important to an organization fulfilling its mission that price should be no obstacle in finding *the* right person. Here are some useful tips on what to watch for and watch out for in deciding whether to use headhunters for your job search:

1. Have you clarified in a paragraph of fifty words or less what the job *is?* Headhunters, who know your business, can help think through (at a price, to be sure) what it is you really need. To this extent, headhunters are management consultants. Business healers. But if you know what you want (the hardest job in filling a job), think through whether you need a headhunter at all.

2. Do you have the time? A headhunter goes to work full-time for you and your organization. Like an accounting house hired to straighten out your deplorable bookkeeping or a law firm to protect you from yourself, specialized headhunting services save you money, time, and worry while you tend to minding the store. A central thesis of this book, however, is that the main function of organizational leadership is the hiring, managing, and firing of key people, the process of which is a necessary growth experience, a lesson you won't learn abdicating this role to an outside consultant.

3. Do you have the money?

Headhunters are expensive. Many won't work for your organization unless they have an "exclusive": an agreement whereby no other placement firms muscle in on the search. Most bill you on a time and charges basis, like a lawyer (and you know what *they* cost!). And there is no guarantee that they will find the right person.

Points to remember:

1. Headhunters often send through three or four candidates unsuitable for your job before Mr. Clean is introduced. This makes a headhunter's best candidate seem all the better.

2. Headhunters can clock horrendous bills. Best a cutoff point. Folly to retain services not producing what you want.

3. Never rely on headhunters to do the background checkout on candidates; they obviously can't ask the kind of questions you can. Insist on *personally* following up your own checkout.

4. Watch out for headhunters who churn your account. Headhunters are hired to *discriminate*. A sure sign of a bad headhunter is when he calls you four times a week with four candidates you *must* see. The chances are good he is on a fishing expedition and picking any slip out of the hat. Like pinning the tail on the donkey, he is wearing a blindfold. The best headhunters don't waste your time—when they want you to see someone, you know your time is well spent.

5. Check out your headhunter's honesty. After interviewing each candidate he sends, frankly tell him what you think of the man or woman. Get his response. Does he sometimes disagree?

"Telling the client what he wants to hear" is the conventional wisdom. The best management consultants sometimes tell clients what they *don't want* to hear. The effective headhunter is more interested in doing a good job than banking a big fee.

6. Has his firm performed other management services for your organization?

Good.

The more background the better.

He knows your players, has a hunch about your hidden agendas, and feels comfortable on the turf. That means he can take a photograph of the firm for his best job candidates. That means the people he sends through your interview hoops have the confidence of his knowledge.

7. Are you prepared to tell the truth about this job?

Everything.

Why four people have filled this job in the past five years, why this division's profit margins have slipped, what managers wield power, etc.

Headhunters need *all* the important information about a job. Full disclosure!

Holding back information out of embarrassment or a false sense of confidentiality is wasting money and a headhunter's time. An effective headhunter is never *emotionally* involved with his clients: He is clinical, objective, and free to give the best advice possible. The sound of an ax grinding is the last thing you're likely to hear from a good headhunter. Moreover, because he has seen and heard the *Sturm un Drang* in so many organizations, nothing is likely to shock him.

8. Did you check out your headhunter?

A few phone calls to his clients are in order.

Headhunters are most useful to small- or medium-size firms with the good sense not to waste money on a top-heavy personnel department. Such organizations fill two or three key jobs a year. These firms save precious overhead dollars by *not* losing money on unnecessary staff functions and use the savings to hire headhunters for key search assignments. For the annual cost of one high-priced personnel clerk, a firm can retain a headhunter for two months to help in filling a hard-to-fill post. It makes dollar sense.

Larger firms and the conglomerates should set up recruitment divisions staffed by headhunters with previous line responsibility: a search consultant to its own firm. In down periods, when no hiring is done, a headhunter is used as an in-house management consultant. Moreover, why not use your home-grown headhunter to help other firms? Nothing in law says you can't help your competition for a fee. It's a way of augmenting organizational capability and increasing trade contacts.

"Don't headhunters specialize?"

Yes.

So choose firms that know the petroleum field if you hire for Atlantic Richfield.

Again, make sure the person who works on your account knows the field. Never hire the firm, always the man or woman who is going to do the work.

Make him or her give examples of (1) similar search assignments he or she has pursued in the past five years and (2) his or her success rate.

"What about flat fees instead of time and charges?"

It could cost your firm 25 per cent of the annual salary of the person your search firm finds.

A good arrangement. Some firms, like my own, might work on this basis. On especially tough recruitment problems, the time-and-charges approach is preferred. It prevents headhunters from being ripped off by clients who can't make up their minds about a job or even whether to fill it. An expensive waste of a headhunter's time.

"How important is confidentiality in the job search?"

Never contact a current employer of a candidate until you have the candidate's permission.

Always advertise your job opening widely inside the organization where you work. If you don't, the chances are good that you are playing bad politics, trying to "control" the placement, a charade of clandestinity worthy of many declining organizations.

Cryptoconfidentiality and Masonic oaths of secrecy do not distinguish an effective headhunting effort.

"What about using want ads?"

Great for herdhunting expeditions.

But learn how to read a résumé: The postal people send you a sack of mail every A.M. that keeps two full-time readers employed.

"Should my organization spend money for a candidate's travel expenses to an interview?"

Travel money for key candidates for important jobs is an important part of your recruitment budget. A lot of people know this fact. When in demand, they like to rip off a free trip to the West Coast to interview for a job they really don't want. If your organization has branch offices or even professional relationships (bankers call them "correspondent relationships"), you would be wise to call upon these out-of-town associates to do your initial interviewing. The point is that these people take a reading on whether the candidate is effective and judge whether there are compelling reasons to fly your tiger to Seattle first class. The money savings are considerable, and it's another way of coalescing relationships with people "out there" whom you don't talk to enough. It's also refreshing to have an outsider's opinion.

"What about letting the key person doing the hiring do the traveling?"

Another way to keep costs down is to let the chief off the reservation. A week's swing to interview ten prospects is a lot cheaper than bringing them to you. And it's good to see candidates on *their* turf—nowhere near as uptight as a formal interview in the home office. Moreover, if you really want to put the recruitment make on a good man or woman, there is no more flattering gambit.

It's another example of what many employers too often forget: Interviewing is a two-way street; the organization's being interviewed, too. So when you *recruit* effective people, go to them.

Some tips for the traveling man:

1. Carefully screen people *on the blower.* You'll know after a half-hour long-distance conversation whether it's worth flying to Philly.

2. Four interviews per day on the road is a maximum. Cramming your schedule puts you off your feed and takes the sheen off your pitch. Remember, your job is to bring home the ivory, not a case of battle fatigue.

3. Never make a job offer while traveling, even if you're certain to offer the job at a later date. Bring your trophy to New York, or wherever your organization celebrates the great laying on of hands; have your prospect make the necessary jump shots in front of your best people—the people whose judgment you trust.

4. A recruiting trip is never mixed with other company business. Too many other pressing matters in Minneapolis diffuse the focus on the all-star cast assembled to hear your earful. Time and time again, as a headhunter, I've seen CEOs give recruitment second or third priority. Dumb—because ten to one, it's the absence of the right man or woman in a vital slot that's causing his weekend workload. Putting first things first means putting people you need first.

5. Have a good time. First-class travel and accommodations, not to impress the candidates so much as yourself. A bad recruiting

trip is always underfinanced; the principal feels like a spear carrier, stage left, when in fact he is the *Heldentenor,* stage center.

"So you want a variety of viewpoints about a candidate?"

That's why you want to run your best candidates by the man or woman in your department who disagrees with you about everything except maybe the weather outside. Both your value systems are so useless that the very least you can do is checkmate each other and as a result come up with a free-formed decision—which is to say an opinion ruthlessly free from both your prejudices and consonant with organizational objectives.

"How do you evaluate interview comments?"

Interview comments are feedback from people who can correct your bad case of people astigmatism.

Need-to-know and need-to-approve players constitute a series of interviewers who offset each other, and together their comments provide a balanced picture for you to review *before* making the decision to hire/not to hire.

Again: Never read interview comments of other interviewers before seeing the candidate yourself. That's contaminating your opinion and prejudging the verdict.

Most comments are *ad hominen,* self-serving, and more a reflection of the interviewer than the interviewee. So read between the lines and at the same time take a reading of the interviewer: His comments are an excellent insight into his own fouled-up perceptions.

Some comments I remember:

"I love the guy; hire him *now*—I want to work for him."

"I wouldn't hire this guy to chalk the yardlines much less be our next business manager."

"This guy is a Ph.D. systems analyst and talks like a barber college graduate."

"First Thomas Edison, then Henry Ford, finally Bob McNamara —now Harvey Mohair—yeah! Hire him!"

Insist that your interviewers give *reasons* for the go/no-go decision. Cheers and jeers are not enough.

Destroy all interview comments once your person is on board.

The idea that these comments could become part of a person's permanent "personnel record" gives me an Orwellian chill.

"What about saving time and convening a panel to interview your candidates in one swoop?"

Then chances are you work for an organization where there are too many players and too small a court. The idea of letting a gaggle of candidates confront your organization's Politburo suggests itself. The panel interview . . . or if you are a job candidate yourself, Murder, Inc.

College presidents, foundation executives, key government officials, and team-oriented business types often are chosen in this manner. Not the best way to pick people. Better the longer, infinitely more personal approach of letting each candidate interview each need-to-approve VIP.

Why?

No matter where, *groups* develop a dynamic adverse to the recruitment process. Nobody can work for a group. That's why the mortality rate among the few chief executive officers reporting to a *working* board of directors is so high. Boards that set and implement policy are by definition racked with contradictions, rivalries, hidden agendas, and suppressed policy conflicts. An important job candidate faced with this kind of collective taffy pull might opt out of a job altogether, or win the support of a bare majority of the board and spend the next two years fending off those who never wanted to hire him in the first place. And, of course, group decisions invariably imply compromise, which is fatal to good health within organizations.

The individual interview causes each interviewer to react to each candidate as a human being. A reciprocity between two people is possible, but between a person and a group, what could have been a beautiful dialogue between equals ends up like an awkward performance of "Meet the Press." The Socratic dialectic of the separate interview is far better than a collective cross-examination.

Moreover, skillful politicians among your candidates often manipulate groups of people but are stonewalled in an individual encounter.

Finally, committees by definition botch the accountability factor, which is paramount in all management decisions. About the only responsibility for most boards of directors is the hiring and firing of the chief executive officer. Don't extend this policy vertically throughout your organization.

"What's wrong with compromise?"

Two department heads must agree on a key person for an important job.

Three candidates are in the running: Department head *A* thinks candidate No. 1 is the cat's meow; department head *B* would put his hand in the fire for candidate No. 2. Both are high on No. 3, but neither sees him as first choice.

Solution?

Hire the third man or woman, and all three live happily ever after.

Wrong, dummy.

Both managers avoided an obviously creative conflict resolution. Both opted for a human relations solution. Both are secretly sorry. Moreover, lack of enthusiasm makes it impossible for candidate No. 3 to enlist the wholehearted support of either. His days are numbered at Sticky Wicket, Inc., because whatever divided the two men in the choice of a third is not resolved; a chance to ratify organizational objectives or change them is lost because people did not fight for their convictions.

Moral?

Never compromise on people.

Either carry the day and hire the man or woman you *want,* or if, after marshaling all your facts, presenting the evidence in the most logical and persuasive manner possible, you are faced down by other facts or the politics of the situation, surrender with grace and prepare to work with the *other* person's superstar.

"Doesn't that make it sticky for the new man or woman when he comes aboard?"

It doesn't have to happen.

If you lose on your first choice, your first responsibility is to have a heart-to-heart with the new man or woman and let that person know, in your estimation, that there was a better person for the job. Doing the responsible thing, clearing the air of the smell of gunpowder after the battle is fought and lost, far from discomfiting the new hired gun, wins his respect. I'll bet he'll knock himself out to prove you wrong. A great day, a few months later, sitting disarmingly on the corner of A's desk, you acknowledge that his was the *right* decision. That's the kind of exchange too rare in organizational life today and the kind of colloquy made possible because neither party to the transaction was prepared to compromise.

The trouble with compromise solutions—not only in choosing people, but also on a whole range of management choices—is that *accountability* for decision-making is blurred; no one takes the blame or wins a kudo. Management by committee is the triumph of groupthink over individual conviction.

Ah, back to basics: The effective manager is the big man or woman who confesses mistakes, the manager who automatically wins the loyalty of his staff, the admiration of *his* boss, and the respect of his colleagues. It's worth an occasional bout with insomnia and executive heartburn.

"Can't you have too many need-to-approve people?"

Indubitably.

I remember once signing off on the hire of a key but middle-level person who required the approval of *seven* other people in the office—I worked harder on finding, scheduling, checking out, interviewing, and winning approval of this candidate than a score of more important jobs I brokered within the organization. The upshot was that nine outstanding candidates passed inspection— none of whom were hired because of collective nitpicking by my colleagues. In desperation, our working group finally agreed on a lovely, competent woman, a paragon of what we, the group, wanted. She lasted 2½ months: The interview process so intimidated her that she froze on the job. Wisely packing her bags, she went back to Carmel, California, where she lived happily ever after.

"Well, if individual interviews by board members or key people in an organization is the best selection method, the scheduling process and staff backstopping seem to me very important."

Filling an important job is full-time employment. Somebody needs to work at it eight hours a day—a headhunter, an ace on your staff, your recruitment division, your special assistant, or even you. You should be satisfied with seeing no less than four key candidates a week—if your time limit is four weeks to fill the job.

The interview time with each candidate is time-consuming enough, but it's also a time for education, candidate comparison, and reflection on how the job can change to fit your favorite candidate. Therefore, to generate four productive interviews a week, somebody is going to have to work full-time generating résumés, tapping the hidden manpower pool, setting up interviews with your need-to-know people, and riding herd on you to *clarify what it is you want*. So the moral is: Assign the donkey work involved in a job search to someone you trust, to write the copy for mass mailing (if you go the public route), develop a "rolling" telephone campaign of knowledgeable sources of candidates, schedule interviews, secure interview comments, and update the job's real objectives.

Time is important to job candidates, too. So if you really spot *the* man or woman to fill your job, don't spin wheels. Often organizations that care the most (that is, that act with decisiveness and speed) are able to capture the best talent. Dilatory organizations, usually ponderous government agencies and blue-chip neanderthals, lose out because of bureaucratic lethargy. For an outfit like yours, all hustle and efficiency, don't waste time on other candidates when you have what turns you on.

"What about overlapping on important jobs?"

Don't do it.

A new man or woman on the job wants his predecessor looking over his shoulder for the next three months ("while he learns the ropes") about as much as I want to share my bed with an incubus.

Like compromise, overlapping never works. Both parties suffer from enormous control problems, each inhibits the other, and both bend over backward to please. Result: sure-fire displeasure for both persons.

The Navy does the job right: A new captain is piped on board, there is a touching ceremony on the rear deck commemorating the change in command. Then the old skipper, with a jaunty salute to Old Glory, marches down the gangplank and off to his next post.

"What about campus recruitment for entry-level job candidates?"

Still a popular recruitment pastime among the industrial giants but hardly necessary for institutions thriving within the competitive market economy.

Business schools are the most popular entrepôt. MBAs by the half ton are poker chips to scores of corporate crapshooters brought in to bag their quota for the headhunting season. But, again, three out of four MBAs leave their first job within two years from graduation. Campus recruitment is cost-defective. The huge investment in time, training, and money used to gull the best and brightest products of America's business schools to sign on for a lifetime voyage with Standard Products, Inc., is for naught.

"So you don't approve of campus recruitment programs?"

No, these programs are bad for organizations and people.

Bad for people because job candidates never learn the necessary arts of wending their way into the job stream, and bad for organizations because they necessarily recruit those whose experience is limited to a curriculum of graduate-school careerism, model-building, and policy analysis. The young are conditioned to expect far more from a job than any organization—even one as big as General Motors—can supply. On both parties' part, there is a massive failure of expectations—thus the general unhappiness of most graduates on their first entry-level job and the high turnover rate within big organizations.

"Why do large organizations continue to recruit on campuses?"

Because organizations, the larger they become, tend to resemble one another in kind *and* degree. And huge organizations are notorious copycats. Let their competition develop an independent R&D branch, and as sure as the sun rises in the east, three of its largest competitors will do the same. Each institution fearing others will steal a march, each justifying their own ill-conceived projects based on actions of their competition.

Recruitment programs grow to resemble one another, which is another major flaw. A systematic recruitment campaign should be based on how one institution differs in kind from another, on how opportunities, let's say, at the Defense Intelligence Agency are qualitatively different—particularly in the caliber of work assignments —than at the Central Intelligence Agency.

• Why work as an international lending officer is more satisfying and more professionally fulfilling at Chase Manhattan than at the Bank of America.

• Why Peat, Marwick, Mitchell & Company offers line CPA assignments with more responsibility leading to a greater sense of professional growth than, say, Lybrand, Cooper. And so on, and so on . . .

The work, time, and planning intelligence are worth it in dollars and cents because they insure finding people who really want work with Consolidated Utilities. What's more appropriate: Hiring a hundred management trainees to staff a large corporation's executive intern program with the chance that ten will actually be promoted a decade later into the executive suite? Or carefully programming ten jobs with real responsibilities—budgets to manage, people to fire, results that can be measured—and selecting the best ten young people who show up at your plant gates and have the gumption to ask for a job?

My bet is on the latter every time. The cost savings alone are impressive, and the gain in quality people is phenomenal—because, of the ten hired via this route, five will make it, as surely as the sun sets in the west, to executive Valhalla.

Corporations should try this approach. The key is to program real jobs where the candidate senses a challenge for achievement and excellence the first day on the job. Arouse these instincts, and firms can forget all the bushwa about retirement plans, benefits, stock options, high salaries, and gimcrack job titles.

Too often, major companies spot the best talent in business school and lock them into nonjobs or into corporate training programs. But grad students, no matter at what level of competence or subject matter, have a secret loathing of training, education, and classroom game playing. People have a great thirst for real work and want to be tested, which management intern programs fail to take into account.

Hire an MBA and tell him "Get us some accounts—now!" He will love you for it.

"Well, what's a better way to recruit collegians if they don't come to your plant gates?"

A mailing service will sell you four hundred names of graduating MBAs or engineers or lawyers or liberal arts types from a score of schools. Send a letter and *describe ten real jobs* you want to fill. *Don't* include a lot of fancy recruitment literature chockablock with glossy photos of young, bright people falling all over each other on their way to the executive dining room.

Don't include any information on salary, benefits, and, so help me Hannah, retirement programs.

Don't offer to pay travel expenses.

Tell as much about each job as possible, especially the challenging aspects. Give the name of operating people doing the interviewing. No one in campus recruitment or personnel, please.

Of ten such letters sent to a typical college, I'll bet that after a week the letter is dog-eared. Total cost to your firm: three hundred dollars plus postage and stationery.

"But my organization would no more give up campus recruitment than it would the morning coffee break. Who should be the campus recruiters?"

Many organizations are no longer detailing campus recruitment to young people, themselves only two or three years away from graduate school.

No, campus recruitment programs, if your organization *won't* learn, are best led by senior-level department heads, persons who have climbed near the top of the corporate heap—where young people, anxious to be accepted to U. S. Steel's Loop Program, expect to be themselves in twenty years. Most of them make far more impressive recruiters than callow youths, who are assigned because they project the company's image rather than its substance. Moreover, these annual swings for senior-level types are like an academic sabbatical, an excellent feedback mechanism on the changing times—nobody's generation gap is going to show if a once-a-year swing is made through ten business schools in the Midwest.

Most campus recruitment is done in the wrong environment—to go to Connossus, when Connossuns should hitchhike to Rome. Campus environments are unreal. No campus recruiter (no matter how persuasive) can reproduce the work environment that prevails at a branch office, say, of Warner-Lambert. True, the follow-up second interview is usually conducted back on industrial turf. But the college graduate who takes the Greyhound to Pittsburgh and checks out Allegheny Steel on his own time and money is more impressive than all the student aristocrats who go shopping with campus recruiters come the first swallow of spring.

And that's the core of the problem.

Most campus recruitment campaigns are shopping expeditions, finding the best "deal"—a decadent Persian Garden where people are not quite put on blocks and made to disrobe while the sheiks pinch their flesh, but almost; and for the student's part, instead of zeroing-in on jobs and institutions *they want,* the point of the game is to see how many job offers they can bag.

CHAPTER 7

How to read a person

"So the interview is the most important factor in hiring for growth jobs?"

More important than the résumé, the interview is *less* important than the "checkout." Who are *you* to think, in a one-hour interview, that your impressionistic feelings are a better guide to judging effective people than those who have worked *over, with,* and *for* your hand-picked prima donna?

To hire a résumé is unheard of. But to hire on the basis of an interview is as bad as horoscoping. Always reserve first impressions until the reference check.

One way to save time is to *personally* do the checkout.

No forms, please.

As soon after your interview as possible. When impressions are freshest. Enthusiasm communicates best across a long-distance telephone line. Things to listen for from your candidate's referees:

1. A pause before answering a question.

If someone needs twenty seconds to think before responding to some fairly elementary questions on your part, he is either dissimulating or dumb. What *we think* of other people (which is the substance of gossip, worldwide) is not something we ponder a goodly time about. So if there's a pause, probe.

There's a good chance that you are about to be a victim of corporate benevolence—that is, the referee is *too* kind; sure, Harry Hotshot never worked out at ABC Chemical, but his boss, Lester Hasbeen, doesn't want to wreck Harry's chances of another job.

This kind of false benignity is bad for everyone. Ten to one, if Hotshot was a problem, it could be Lester's fault as much as Harry's.

It doesn't take long to reach the bottom in most intraorganizational squabbles. You owe it to yourself and your organization to find out the truth about why Harry didn't work out at ABC. Maybe he left for the *right* reasons—all the more cause for you to hire someone with a sense of independence and self-esteem.

Beware of the 1,000 per cent endorsement.

Its fishy smell is a warning to ask for the names of other people at ABC Chemical who knew Harry Hotshot, too.

Nobody walks on water.

The best candidates, whether for the secretarial pool or nominees to the board, particularly *the best and the brightest,* suffer from a variety of afflictions. As his employer, you need to know about a candidate's weaknesses because you've sensed his strengths in the interview. Moreover, the information you acquire is a preview of your candidate's on-the-job performance and a splendid hedge against future disappointment.

2. Prepare your questions *in advance*. Make notes. Ask the *same* questions to others who know your candidate. If you still can't detect areas of conjecture, controversy, and weakness, start over. You are not asking the right questions, obviously. Wrong questions elicit useless information. We all think too much in polar extremes. What are those interesting shades of gray you seem to perceive? The black-and-white sketch in a reference checkout is bush league. What you want is a composition in gray subtleties, not a Rorschach blot.

3. Dun & Bradstreet checks out companies; Retail Credit and Pinkerton check out individuals. For important jobs involving fiduciary responsibility, these services are vital. Make it vividly clear to your candidate *why* this special checkout is necessary. Nobody denies that organizations must do some necessary snooping if they are about to invest a good percentage of their profits in somebody; but job candidates need to know and give permission.

4. Check on your telephone voice.

Sure, you can negotiate a twenty-million-dollar mineral rights settlement, in Spanish, for God's sake, on behalf of your Latin American subsidiary, and while checking out a job candidate sound like Andy Hardy on his first date. If you can't, find someone who can!

A headhunter's knack is eliciting information on the phone. Candor, honesty, concision, and precision in your approach—plus a capsule clarification of the flair factors—are what a referee needs to know.

Let the referee do the talking. Your job is to interrupt with *follow-up* questions, the kind of questions our former President was never asked at his infrequent press conferences.

5. Don't hesitate to call back a referee. Most referees are delighted to talk about *what they know about:* a big change from the flibberty-gibberty puzzles most of us face every workday. People like to talk about something they know about for a change.

6. Don't cave in when your highest expectations of someone collapse. It's because (1) your expectations are too high anyway, (2) the person is your *only* candidate, or (3) the whole business is too much work. Shame on you. And you bill at the rate of thirty dollars an hour.

"Corporate benevolence, true. But don't many managers try to kill off job chances with next employers?"

Paranoia.

Found widely among the long-term unemployed. It's mostly in their minds. Of course, that's where all our problems are. Getting at the trouble is the first responsibility of the jobless who sense Fate is pointing its fickle finger at them.

Sure as shootin', if you are black, female, a Viet vet, a CO, not a college graduate, a Ph.D., an older person, Jewish, Spanish-speaking, and/or if you are coping with a first-class case of the white-collar jobless blues, you are projecting the blame on someone other than yourself.

That's one reason why firing people responsibly is so important —why the exit interview where you learn the real reason you're cashiered is vital. And if this fate should befall you, the very least management should do is tell you exactly what they are going to tell your next potential employer. Not to do so is to leave someone with a bad case of the paranoia bends.

No official party line; no formal letter of discharge. Someone at Sticky Wicket, Inc., must answer for Johnny Appleseed, who didn't make the team. That means knowing what Johnny did *right* as well as where he failed.

Balanced reporting on people is a manager's foremost responsibility to the departed executive. The formal, official termination notice, leaving unsaid everything the next employer should know about John, babe, is the kiss of death. Too little information or damning with faint praise is the cause of most unemployed people's paranoia.

I once hired a three-time-fired person who worked out very well. The checkout revealed he was fired for the right reasons, reasons that supported the flair factors needed to do the new job.

"Well, suppose a candidate is supereffective in what he does and for what you want him to do, but doesn't possess other desirable characteristics?"

Stick to the flair factors. Do they mesh with the job? If so, you have your man or woman; grab on and hold tight!

Don't make Lincoln's mistake.

Item: Of eight speechwriters I hired, four journalists, two novelists, a college dropout, and a drunk, the last two were least "qualified." Guess which two were most effective?

Item: I once hired ten schoolteachers for an important contract; the three most effective *never* taught school before.

Item: Of the five truly great entrepreneurs I know, none went to business schools.

Item: Of eight great college presidents I know, one has no college degree and five others lack a Ph.D., and none had been a college president *before.*

Items: The best top sergeant I knew in the Army never went to NCO school, my best college professor never published a book, and the best economist I know is a lawyer.

Now, this is not to knock economists, or the Ph.D., or the NCO academy, or the value of publishing, or the importance of experience. My point is simple: People are either *effective* or *ineffective* on the job. On the checkout, that's what you want to find out. There are plenty of effective college presidents with Ph.D.s, first-rate NCOs who attended the NCO academy, excellent professors who publish, top-flight speechwriters who are journalists, and effective economists who attended the Wharton School. But their badges are not proof that they are *effective.*

"Do people lie about themselves in an interview?"

More downright mendacity is exchanged between employer and potential employee than in any other social situation known to man, save sexual seduction. When people go job hunting the downright, doggone, deep bayou country lying that goes on is truly mind bending.

And all the lying isn't found only on the part of the job candidate, hat-in-hand, best-foot-forward, the world-is-my-oyster profile. No, whether they represent the go-go semiconductor industry, a hotshot new government alphabetic agency, or a new and swingin' progressive institution of higher learning, employers start swapping lies with their interlocutors to the point that the air is blue with the b.s. factor.

Whether you hire or want to hire yourself an employer, always tell the truth.

"How can you tell when a candidate is telling the truth?"

When there is no inconsistency among his (1) résumé, (2) interview, and (3) reference checkout.

A lot of answers flow from the candidate's referees, information that ratifies, differs with, or plays no role in what the candidate told *you*. Reference checkouts complete an authentic profile of your candidate: How well did he know himself in comparison with those who know him and his work best?

Factual discrepancies between a candidate's résumé and interview presentation in comparison with the referee's report could be enough to reject a candidate forthwith. There can be *no* business relationship (and the whole job-placement process is a business relationship) between one party who tells the truth about a job (*you*) and another who enjoys exercises in mendacity. No faith or trust, central to our whole credit economy ("I agree to pay you such-and-such an amount for the following product or service" obtains), because one party to the deal is dishonest—with himself as much as with you.

That's why knowing what you want; describing a job accurately, warts and all; and hazarding a definition of the flair factors inspire the kind of trust your best candidates admire. Being candid, the essence of productive relationships, is your guarantee that your best candidates will be open, too.

Other signs a candidate is lying or omitting the truth:

1. No eye contact.
2. Irregular voice intonation.
3. Chinese answers.
4. Constricted body language.

If a candidate knows "all the answers," never says "I don't know," watch out! Who has *all* the answers, these days, to anything?

"What about interviewing people with a view to identifying character traits important to perform the job?"

You mean, like intelligence, honesty, flexibility?

Hopeless in picking people for important jobs on a specific basis. Remember Lincoln's problems!

Doing so is simply adding another layer of horse manure on top of a humus pile so rich it's likely to explode from spontaneous combustion.

In picking people, diagraming personal value systems is to tie your hands.

I never use interview rating sheets.

"So you oppose the use of interview grading forms. Does that apply to performance review, efficiency, or 'fitness' reports?"

The only forms in a company I wholly approve of are the W-2 forms for the Internal Revenue Service and monthly productivity reports kept on everyone from the chairman of the board to the PBX operator. The useful existence of every other form is seriously debatable.

Interview forms resemble the following:

INTERVIEW REPORT

Rate the interviewee on a scale of 1 to 5.
1: Poor   2: Fair   3: Good   4: Excellent   5: Superior
Circle only one

Technical skill	1	2	3	4	5
Flexibility	1	2	3	4	5
Intelligence	1	2	3	4	5
Alertness	1	2	3	4	5

Ability with people	1	2	3	4	5
Appearance	1	2	3	4	5
Aggressiveness	1	2	3	4	5

In reality, of course, these forms are longer, more "sophisticated," and hopelessly unreal in helping you pick better people. Performance review reports are the same: longer, more complex graduation schemes, space for narrative and subjective evaluation encouraged. I've seen performance review reports that invite a supervisor to rate everything from the way his subordinate holds a cocktail to "his coolness under fire" to the social adaptability of his wife.

Crap.

Pardon my French, but the tiresome dumbness of rating people with checkmarks in little boxes is enough to paralyze my pineal gland and block my bile duct.

In performance rating for you, as the "boss," to play God with your "subordinate's" performance, to become trapped by bureaucratic rating forms *prepared by someone else,* is to abdicate the special relationship that exists between you and every other human being. And that special bond is something that must be evaluated *together.*

In other words, all mandatory performance evaluation (which is important) should be conducted in an informal setting. There should —at the outset—be nothing written. It should be a discussion between two human beings. And you, the official "superior," can learn as much as you teach; the mutuality of exchange is what is important, for you, too, are being evaluated—every minute of the day by the people you lead. Listening to what they say is the first, most important, step to real leadership.

Second, after an initial discussion, write a report—and let its subject review it. Some organizations have experimented with people writing their own evaluations, which is not enough, but a useful supplement to the report you write.

Third, in conducting evaluations for all the people who report to you, query everyone about each other—peer evaluation is useful as an information-gathering device about your division as a whole.

Fourth, ask for a frank opinion of your man or woman from those people at your level in the organization who have occasion to work closely with the person in question.

All four sources of information—(1) yourself, (2) the employee, (3) his peers, and (4) other key managers—will give a synoptic view of how *effective* his performance is on the job. Mesh all this information into a final report and use this information in a final conversation with the man or woman under evaluation.

As for interviewing, forget trying to rate personal "characteristics." Stick to what is wanted in the job. What are the flair factors required? That's putting first things first. And who the hell cares:

• if your foreign-exchange expert has the personality of a camel driver, if he knows arbitrage inside and out.

• if your speechwriter is a weekend drunk but can knock out an airport rally address in twenty minutes on a portable typewriter on his lap while you both wait to land at Logan International.

• if your financial planning chief's politics are five hundred miles right of Calvin Coolidge if he can project project costs for the next fiscal year within 5 per cent.

Choosing people on the basis of general acceptability, actually adding up numbers—everything from test scores to personality inventories to interview scorecards—and then offering a key job to someone who scores ninety plus is certain to disappoint you in your candidate, and the candidate in your organization, because neither party is focused on the *task* to be done. That's why so many people of potential never finally flower. Everyone is so much like everyone else it's like you were trapped in a house of mirrors.

"What happens when you've finally settled on offering a key job, and then new information about your lead person completely botches the match up?"

Item: Your organization is searching for a chief executive officer, and your best candidate is revealed to have a history of coronary heart disease.

Item: You are about to promote a whiz of a finance type to take charge of your company's internal audit; the Pinkerton report states he spends every fourth weekend in Las Vegas.

Item: A plant manager's job in northern Ireland is a short-fuse operation; your best candidate once took a leave of absence because of psychiatric problems.

It's the typical fisherman's refrain: the tale of the one that got away. Every duck was lined up, salary, dates, responsibilities, approval of need-to-know people et al., only to have the whole beautiful relationship befouled in the last hour.

If ever speed was of the essence, now is the time to work hard and long on the blower to pin down the facts, to engage the best and wisest minds within your organization, and to face up to sometimes brutal decisions. Never leave someone to "twist slowly in the wind," quoting John Ehrlichman. To do so is inhuman and a triumph of process over people.

What do you do?

1. Phone or talk with your candidate *immediately*. No need to reveal your sources. They are as sacrosanct as a journalist's.

2. What is the candidate's version? Be sure to take notes. A verbatim transcript might be in order. So don't hesitate to tell him your steno is taking notes and listening on a third line. This is a serious situation.

3. Ask for the names and numbers of people who verify *his* version or who shed qualifying information.

4. Prepare an oral report and discuss it on a need-to-know basis, particularly with that person who has operational responsibility for the job. The subject deserves interrupting people on vacation, breaking up a meeting, and waiting to see those who need to know long past quitting time.

5. Why wasn't this information revealed in the course of his interviews?

Crucial.

Remember the Eagleton affair? The veracity of your candidate—his character—is much more important than the objective facts—the nervous condition, a gambling propensity, the heart condition.

6. If your key man or woman *lied,* drop him, pronto. And tell him why; that way he learns that those who can't face important information about themselves or refuse to share it with those who need to know are candidates for nothing except unemployment compensation.

7. Extenuating circumstances? Find out the complete story and weigh whether to keep his candidacy alive. After all, a CEO with a heart condition is surely nothing new, practically a qualification! The same goes for other information—maybe your finance type goes to Vegas to visit an ex-wife and the kids. As for your candidate with a psychiatric history, many people seek mental care as a prophylactic,

to become stronger people, not because they are candidates for the booby hatch.

8. Once a decision is reached, any decision, communicate it verbally to the candidate. Tell the truth—no Chinese dialogue.

9. Never offer him another, secondary, job. Come down hard either for hire or strong for breaking off the relationship. No half-assed compromises.

10. If the answer is "No," a telephone call from you with the *real* reasons is necessary. Not calling back is rude, cowardly, and bad form. These are never easy calls to make, but yours is not a nonjob job, is it?

"What are the kinds of questions you ask referees?"

There is only one real question: *"Is this person effective?"*

Don't ask whether he's a "nice" person, whether he drinks *too* much, how well he gets along with people, his politics, his clubs, and all the rest.

And who cares if the guy or gal you want to hire is loyal, obedient, punctual, courteous, flexible, courageous, hard-working, intelligent, energetic, or fair?

What you want to know, goddamnit, is: Is he *effective?* If there is hesitation on this point, move on to your next candidate. Don't make Lincoln's mistake; find someone to march South—now.

"First impressions are very important in my business. Isn't a candidate's appearance vital in the first interview?"

You can't tell it from a résumé; but you can judge appearance roughly the first fifteen seconds of an interview, which is decisive in the minds of plenty of employers. "I didn't like his looks" is an expression I've heard from a score of employers who are otherwise fairly rational about major decisions. Why is appearance so important? And so unimportant? In our mind's eye we establish what a person should look like for a job, even though we know it's nonsense. How otherwise do you explain the uniform looks of advertising executives, industrial consultants, and marine drill sergeants?

To test this theory out, I conducted an experiment. My company was simultaneously hiring for four different contracts. All of them differed in scope of work, objectives, and types of manpower. Of more than a hundred people I talked with over a four-week period, I could spot, by quickly glancing across the waiting room, which person was a candidate for which contract. The four kinds of jobs included (1) academics, (2) inner-city community action types, (3) system analysts, and (4) political action people.

There was no particular prescience on my part; anyone could have done at least as well. After eight years in the people business, I feel like a casting director.

Sure, appearance is important in up-front growth jobs. But I've hired plenty of effectives who needed hosing-down, too. Of course, we always keep them in the back room with the lawyers.

"Should there be a lot of competition for a good job?"

Lots of it these days in the marketplace.

So encourage a great deal more in your job search by letting those in your department compete, too. They themselves might qualify or have sources of candidates you can tap.

Growing organizations still look long and hard for good people despite the oversupply in most manpower pools.

Effective people are always hard to find.

"Why are so many employment interviews blahsville?"

That's when an employer doesn't know what he wants or, if he does, what flair factors are necessary.

Or when the job seeker, not knowing what he wants, tries to fathom what's available.

When interviews fail, it's because the answers to the following questions don't mesh:

Employer: "What is to be done?"
Applicant: "What do I want to do?"
Employer: "What flair factors are necessary for the job?"
Applicant: "Do I have what it takes?"

"Why are answers to these questions so important?"

Well, for openers, most employers:

1. Don't focus on organizational objectives and therefore can't zero-in on who they want or why.

2. Don't know where they are going and therefore don't know how to get there.

3. Choose people on the whimsical basis of habit ("we've always had an inventory chief") or allow the "experts," the company healers, to tell them what they need.

The most important reason an interview aborts is that one or both parties *want* it to fail—that is, unless both parties consciously or unconsciously wants what the other has, the interview flops.

I've flunked interviews, and I've flunked plenty of interviewees. Looking inward and checking against many who talk to me about their interview misfires, what's strikingly common is that people, whether employers or applicants, unconsciously "blow" an interview, one or both parties to a bad interview *make* it fail.

"How do you manage interviews where clearly the first five minutes suggest no deal is possible?"

Those interviews where:

- you interview your boss's spastic nephew.
- the candidate has already accepted another job.
- the résumé didn't match the candidate.
- your job order has been canceled.

There are a thousand reasons.

Courtesy interviews.

Again, most headhunters never interview anyone for less than an hour. My "courtesy interviews" last no longer than ten minutes. If clearly no business can be transacted—no matter the candidate was flown in from the West Coast—the point of the discussion is to drop the gate—fast.

Ruthless?

Not in the least—nothing is as false and uptight as an aborted business meeting. An interview, for example, for a job you don't have. Swapping lies and golf lore during business hours with a job candidate is like a three-hour lunch with a sales prospect whose company that morning went into receivership.

I always remember the names of men and women I've interviewed who take the initiative and terminate my interview quickly. The next time I call them, we won't be wasting each other's time.

"What about testing job applicants with hypothetical problem-solving situations in an interview situation?"

A favorite pastime of many employers. Of course, it doesn't work.

Hypothetical case-solving in interview situations is ivory towerism; it certifies model builders, theoreticians, and business intellectuals—which is O.K. if you are hiring for a think tank, a college faculty, or the Harvard *Business Review:* Such tactics do reveal intelligence and logical intellectual processes.

Far better, in the practical business of hiring, to make interviewees focus on *real* problem-solving from their own occupational and personal lives. What this disquisition lacks in elegance it compensates for in realism, and it lets employers make the imaginary jump from the interview to the workshop.

"How many people have you fired and how?"

"What social science techniques did you use to perform this longitudinal study?"

"What are examples of the principles of community development you applied on your last three jobs?"

"Where did you put your convictions on the line?"

Make interviewees give real answers to real questions from the real world. That's letting a job applicant take a photograph of himself—warts and all. Let the imagists and model builders keep their halos and Rockefeller grants.

"How do you screen out the 'yes' men?"

Develop two or three lines of divergence in an interview situation so that a healthy disagreement can take place. This tests your candidate's ability to think on his feet, his "social" security, independence of mind, and intellectual honesty. What is advocated is a deliberate strategy of disagreement to find out if you're about to hire a "yes" man or woman, or someone with the kind of independence of thought that could lead to self-reliant action, the kind of person you don't need to supervise.

"What about 'stress' interviews?"

Stress interviews are favored by hard-nosed and bone-headed

managers. Like the hypothetical problem-solving interview, the stress interview fosters gamesmanship and role playing. But job interviews never correspond to on-the-job situations. Inducing phony stress factors into an interview violates the essential condition of a business relationship: trust.

"Earlier you said, in a fit of pique, that frustration was part of even a good growth job. How can you spot a candidate who knows about the inevitably boring and defeating aspects of any job—no matter how good?"

If you do a lot of hiring, try to index the frustration quotient of your interviewee. Did this person (and make him give examples) ever work at something that required vastly more brawn than brains, more industriousness than ingenuity, more persistence than perspicacity? Five or six convincing examples of mature behavior in the face of mind-boggling boredom underwrite this person's occupational integrity.

Routine, repetitive, reflexive behavior is a component, a major nucleus of any job, whether president of an engineering firm or the manager of his janitorial services. Learning to live with and being proud of one's coping capabilities, whether it's housewifely chores or working as a space salesman, is the first essential *any* employer should discover in *any* job applicant for *any* job.

"What about when you must fill a job with a specialist in a field you know nothing about?"

Like that assignment of mine to hire a lawyer. Well, any employer with this problem needs help. Someone to assess your candidates functionally; something you can't do.

Your assignment is to find the best data-processing supervisor thirty thousand dollars can buy. You work in line management and often confuse computer languages with Esperanto.

Hire out an expert either in-house or outside who tells you everything you need to know about the candidate's skills. Make your expert stick to what you need; have him focus on the candidate's flair factors. If you use outside resources, a hundred-buck fee for this courtesy is not out of order.

"What kind of people should you avoid hiring no matter what kind of important job you have?"

Asking a general question like that invites me to answer with a glittering half truth.

For example, *in general,* shrewd employers avoid hiring passive, dependent personalities, no matter what their disguises, for important jobs. But for grunt jobs, passive dependents can be just the ticket.

Other things I watch for:

1. Does the candidate bring up salary and fringe benefits *too* early in the interview process, especially—in a job like yours—where the salary is really "open"?

2. Does he seem credentials happy, citing this degree and that certificate as proofs of his paying the admission fee to your field or trade? In a word, is he a sheepskin psychotic?

3. Does your candidate talk to you about his personal needs, or does he have the good sense to make you talk about yours? Amazingly, I've interviewed job candidates who give me a thousand reasons why they *need* a job and mumble not a word about why they *want* one.

If someone says he needs a job for five more years to ensure his retirement, watch out.

If he talks about how he needs to pay his kids' college tuition bills, buyer beware.

If he talks about the inner man being satisfied by work—any kind of work—why doesn't he find it elsewhere?

4. Does your candidate try too hard to please, effuse gratitude, roll over like a cocker spaniel?

5. Is your job candidate looking for his father? Do you have time to be his mentor? Acceptable, perhaps, among those still in their twenties. But immature, to the extreme, in someone who wants a major job in your organization.

6. Does he disagree with you?

7. Did you easily intimidate him?

8. Did he clam up when you asked him to talk about his accomplishments?

9. If not, did he stress merit badges won rather than solid achievements?

10. Does your interviewee try to *control* the interview? Neither party to an interview can control it.

11. Is the job you have in the real self-interest of your candidate to accept? Emotionally disturbed job seekers have trouble being clear-headed about motives. If they don't make sense (even to themselves), how do they help your organization?

12. Why does your candidate want your job? Money, status, publications opportunities, travel, all legitimate needs, to be sure, but hardly, unless you hire for the Ford Foundation, a reason for you to hire him. What does he want to *accomplish?*

13. What are the major *contributions* your candidate can make to your organization? How does your man or woman make your organization qualitatively different and *better?*

If he can survive this enfilade, what are you waiting for? Check him out and sign him up!

"Any other special types?"

Well, two more: subspecies in the general passive/dependent genre.

Hesitate, think twice, and obtain another opinion before hiring someone because he or she is "nice." Liking people is an important part of the people-picking process; how *effective* a candidate is, is more important.

"What's wrong with hiring nice people?"

What are nice people?

In my judgment, they are mostly incompetents.

Nice people are so afraid of failure they never compete (and never against themselves), *castrati* who hate to make decisions. But, *my,* do they know how to "get along." They adapt quickly to the environment and become part of its coloring—the bland leading the bland. Many firms are literally choking on "nice" people—people who don't make demands, don't work for change, don't act unless led. In a word, the vast majority of the human race.

The problem of nice people is easily solved.

Decide that the nicest people in the world are effective people. It might change your whole life!

Do they get the job done?

What you want is an effective, executive environment where ye shall be known by your fruits.

"What's the other type?"

What I call the "good soldier."

Or the man or woman who puts loyalty to your person before family, nation, and God. "Always faithful and constant" is his or her motto.

Of all the overrated "positive" characteristics sought for in key people, loyalty is surely the least understood. And yet it's this particular characteristic—I wager my headhunter's license—that causes more mischief within organizations and produces more disappointment in bottom-line results than any other factor in the whole people-picking process. Examples from corporate, political, and military history abound. Excess loyalty, doglike devotion to the *Führerprinzip,* and irrational abdication of personal responsibility are the root causes of much organizational malfunctioning.

"So choose independent people. Easy."

We pay lip service to independence, but in the clutch, we go with those men and women without any talent except a special predilection for devout homage before the altars of our own personal ambition. When we choose people in this manner, it's our most secret Achilles heel, the weakest point in our own personal Maginot Line.

"I don't understand the difference you make between independent people and individualists."

Rugged individualists are one-man guns, mavericks, and eccentrics. Even a genius here and there. In organizational environments, aloof and noninvolved from people, as most individualists are, they lack the kind of engagement with the environment required in growth organizations, where people are central.

But an independent person is free-acting. Remember?

To act within organizations means working with people. So, while independent personalities are the kind your organization recruits for judgment jobs, it doesn't follow that individualists are wanted.

An independent person, as opposed to the individualist, wants involvement because *it is no burden to his individuality*.

So by all means give special priority to those who challenge the conventional wisdom, who question the canons of your professional expertise, people likely to save yourself from yourself. At the same time, judge whether this candidate for a job is merely an individualist on an ego trip or an independent person who wants real people involvement.

"I thought 'individualism' was a quality we employers always searched out."

Individualism.

Losing its sheen as this century wears on . . . its history, like that of classical free enterprise, a glorious one, but its future these days is dim.

Rugged. Free-spirited. Swashbuckling. Arrogant.

Great qualities still, recruiting entrepreneurs, CIA spooks, and literary critics.

Fatal in professions requiring (and what doesn't these days?) intense personal relationships involving lateral, horizontal, and vertical lines of authority. Often useful to spy in finding chief executive officers, but increasingly rare among CEO candidates. Because the system doesn't encourage individualism any more: Alfred P. Sloan of General Motors; A. P. Giannini of the Bank of America; Harold Ickes at Interior—great individualists all. But would they be hired today by Top Management in the institutions they headed?

Probably not. Tragic? Chalk it up to changing times.

"What's the first question you ask a job candidate?"

First things first: My first question with a fresh job candidate is, "By the way, why were you fired from your last job?"

Sure it's tough, but the question that is hype and a sharp blow to the solar plexus has a way of launching an interview into the most sensitive matters *first*. The answer has no little value in judging the character and candor of a candidate. It helps keep the mendacity quotient to a minimum.

The subject of being fired is held in positive Victorian secrecy by most job candidates and not a few of their former employers. It deserved ventilation at the beginning of this book (rather than at its end) because almost all candidates for employment—no matter how carefully they conceal it from themselves—are leaving one organization for another because of unacceptable dissatisfaction with themselves, the organization for which they work, or the "career" that they pursued.

Almost all candidates for jobs, therefore, are in a transitional stage, psychologically trying to cope with a new set of personal and occupational parameters. And it doesn't matter whether the candidate you interviewed voluntarily quit his last position or terminated his contract or was "riffed" or outright cashiered. Every man and woman in his or her mind is closing out a chapter on the past and beginning a new page of occupational history.

"So it's important to discover why someone quit or was fired from his last job?"

No. Not until you are very, very interested in hiring him.

Interviewers spend altogether too much time trying to find out *why* a candidate was separated from his last employer and nowhere near enough time in probing to find out why the man or woman *wants* work at Amalgamated Industries, Inc. In a word, employers are too interested, practically purient, on the subject of why a candidate left his previous employer, and nowhere curious enough about why he wants an R&D job at Amalgamated. It's like putting the cart before the horse, because employers hire for the present and future—not the past.

Once you've found out the ostensible reason John Q. Jobseek is in your office and why he left Funny Farm, Inc., lead in as to why he wants to work for Amalgamated, Inc. That's where an employer's interests are at stake. And if there appears to be a mesh—that is, there's a job and the man or woman in front of you seems to fit— then come on like a prosecuting attorney as to the candidate's reasons in leaving his past job, once you're satisfied his motives are right for working for you.

"So don't go ransacking a person's past until you're sure he has a shot at a job?"

Right.

Another good reason for this strategy is the time factor. If you spend (and you can lavish an inordinate amount of time hearing the hard-luck stories of a score of untalented candidates) valuable hours talking about the candidate's *past,* you hardly do justice to his pre-

sumptively interesting *future*. Moreover, as every executive employment survey bears out, due to the cyclonic turnover in executive or
judgment jobs, the sheer psycholabor discovering the hidden reason
people leave jobs leaves little time to go to the heart of a person.

So, to keep first things first, concentrate on the present and future.
Let the dead past bury itself. Only when you've focused on one or
two lead candidates is it time to play historical detective.

"Any special difference to the employer between the employed and the unemployed when looking for a job?"

The major difference is that employed candidates have more
chutzpah than their unemployed, down-in-their-luck brothers.

"O.K. What about hiring people already on somebody else's payroll?"

Why are they talking to you if they are intrinsically unhappy in
their current employment?

What do they intend to conceal from you?

Why are they interested in a lateral move to your organization?

Employers need hard answers to these questions. People's hidden
agendas, their real motivations, remember, are the keys to whether
they are going to work out at Amalgamated Industries, Inc.

So let's take first things first and construct a checklist of essentials
you need to know about a job candidate just because he or she *is*
employed:

1. Would your job afford a promotion in comparison with the
candidate's current job in (a) salary, (b) responsibility, and (c)
quality of work?

2. How was the candidate introduced to the job opening; how
did he hear about it?

3. Is your candidate's current job similar to yours in character; is
it in the same field or trade, and above all, is it in the same *functional*
area?

4. How does your candidate *fit* the people he would work for,
with, and under vis-à-vis age, sex, experience, education, temperament, class, and intelligence?

5. What are his reasons for leaving his current position?

6. What are his reasons for wanting to consider your position? Is
he running away from his job?

7. The toughest question of all: What does he *want?* What makes Sammy run, and in what direction? Downfield? Laterally, in the direction of the sidelines? Or even backward—straight to the security of the womb?

"What can you expect from hiring people at the same level of responsibility and pay as their last job?"

The lateral move.

Dangerous, for you and the person who wants the job.

Tough on those who rise fast and finally hit somebody's ceiling. It means all they can do is bump along, like a helium balloon, unless they find a bigger room with a higher ceiling, which means changing fields.

If you are a wise employer, you'll spot a superstar in one field and see his potential in yours.

What happens, in other words, to the college president? Another university?

Or the Cabinet member? The White House?

Or the head of ITT? A&P?

Not likely. Some of us eventually reach the maximum span our talent and field allow. We grow bored with our own accomplishments. Life has no zest; being at the top of your form and the top of your firm can be a real drag. That's when we run for Congress and other pathologies surface. Also, when the Peter Principle, even for the best and the brightest, becomes operative.

"So a person successful in one field is likely to be a success in another?"

Yes, if the person *wants* a job and has the talent to perform it.

The whole process is fascinating. Transiting from one field of accomplishment to another. A great growth experience. And one that is rapidly becoming a common feature in our increasingly dynamic economy and highly mobile job market.

Drawing from a rich manpower pool, managers should choose people who make a habit of success in one field and want to be successful in another. The wise manager goes with proven success, competence, and drive—no matter what the field—rather than lamely falling back on the experiential, educational, and fail factor "qualifications."

Who says a good M.B.A. won't make a fine infantry platoon commander? That a theologian won't work out as a diplomat? That a circus barker can't audition for the "Today" show? Nobody. And everybody. Since all of us have been trained since infancy to believe that there is an organic connection between employment and experience, forgetting that people who make a habit of success know what they want and go after it.

Breaking new ground, new responses to different challenges, the zest for adventure is a much better "qualification" for a job. The Iowa farmer who builds a boat and sails around the world; the U.S. senator who eschews the campaign trail and takes up the ministry; the general who resigns a two-star commission and an Army Corps to set up his own construction firm. Hybriding talent across distinct occupational frontiers produces a new breed.

The risk you take lies only in what other people in the organization think of you. Have the good sense to look behind a person's education and experience at the man himself.

And looking in unusual places to find effective people is how to fill important jobs.

Where I work I see this kind of crosspollination paying off—in spades—all the time.

Our top Mexican-American expert can't speak Spanish; our best financial vice president majored in political science; our boss (my firm is a management services firm) is a trained city manager; our best programmer, an immigrant Englishman; our best project manager, a woman liberal arts major and ex-secretary; our best marketing man, an aeronautical engineer; and so on.

The point is, of course, that trained experts didn't put together, manage, and make our company grow. The work we do doesn't necessarily match up against our résumés—what we were trained to do isn't what we did, and what we did isn't what we are doing.

CHAPTER 8

Face-to-face

"What are some stereotypes you've come across in your hiring experience?"

For openers, the Big Picture man.

"Let me try to bring it all into perspective."

"I'm not so much a detail man as a Big Picture type."

"I paint with broad strokes."

"Bring me nothing but bad news—my shoulders are broad."

These, and many other orotundities like it, come from the lips of self-nominated Renaissance men who despise the nitty-gritty and sound like a Rotarian on an acid trip.

Steer clear of them.

Any leader in no matter what kind of organization who deputizes detail and concentrates on "policy analysis" is a bloated fish at the bottom of the Dead Sea.

Why?

No matter what kind of organization, true leadership involves real work back in the kitchen and down in the boiler room. High policy really can't be made without understanding all the informational inputs that went into its formation. The "nitty-gritty" is organizational policy. No one expects the chief executive officer where you work to *do* the little details so essential in the making of things work. At the same time, they must understand, evaluate, criticize, and make cogent recommendations based on the mountains of staff work that go into important decisions.

Big Picture people have no understanding that great paintings are composed of thousands of infinitesimal details, which must be studied and criticized. Big Picture VIPs are identified by pomposity of speech, writings, and publications (probe to find out whether they employ speechwriters), the dope sheet of their underlings (those

who did the work while the Big Picture people talked about it).
"Peer" and "subordinate" evaluations are quintessential. Most important, what did the marketplace report?

" 'What did the marketplace report?' "

What did the market say?

That is, the population your candidate served; not shareholders, but customers; not alumni, but students; not the commander in chief, but the troops in the field; not necessarily those who hired him, but those *for* whom he was hired.

Carefully check on the real substance of a man as opposed to his image. Screen out Madison Avenue gasbags.

"How can I spot the real self-starters from the pack of dependent passives you say will darken my door?"

In your search for the best people possible, my guess is that you will find far fewer real self-starters than you would think. Everyone interviewed, I'll wager my house mortgage, will modestly admit to being a "self-starter, idea man, doer (not a thinker), innovator," and so forth.

It's up to the skillful interviewer to analyze these sweeping characteriological generalizations into specific and concrete instances of potency, success, and effectiveness. And don't let anyone off the hook; you will be doing, even if you don't hire them to be your next general manager, an enormous service in making them render to Caesar what they so freely confess to God.

"Why is taking risks so important in candidates who would fill judgment jobs?"

Real leadership includes a capacity to make mistakes and learn from them, to risk being *foolish* in the eyes of the world, and to take responsibility for goals greater than one's own: organizational goals. Is the man or woman, therefore, *able* to take risks both in his own life and on the job? The risk-taking capability is that singular factor, so rare among even our best-trained men and women, that is the *sine qua non* of line leadership positions.

"I see your point about the 'Big Picture' people. But what about their opposites?"

The Lilliputians, often experts, consultants, technicians—the people who see a part of the picture but can't grasp the whole. The typical attitude of your average Lilliputian is that his part *is* greater than the whole.

Curiously, among the ranks of the Lilliputians you find some intelligent, able, and competent people. Properly placed in the right jobs, they are simply invaluable. Most occupy judgment jobs. But unless they can overcome the astigmatism that often affects their class, they never advance beyond the specialty jobs to *line* management positions. By line management, we mean highly visible jobs where accountability is entirely in terms of results. Results are vastly more important than *discussion:* the forte of the smart, *little* people in your organization.

People are *little* when they are unable to empathize with or don't want to understand Top Management's position. Above all, they don't want to engage in confrontational involvement with the Big Wheels Upstairs. The Little People, therefore, spend an inordinate amount of time pouting around the water cooler; they flail at Top Management over coffee in the company cafeteria; of a Friday evening, they love to regale their spouses with snafus on the job which, of course, are Higher Authority's responsibility.

In a word, the Little People like their scapegoats to be big, remote, and almost always wrong. The idea of being promoted into the territory of real organizational leadership terrifies them. They would no sooner be the point man in their organization than they would welcome three rounds of fisticuffs with Muhammad Ali.

As we become more specialized and industrialized, there is abundant evidence that the ranks of the Lilliputians are growing. The web they weave is becoming harder for organizational Gullivers to break. Line management needs to identify and neutralize the Little People's propensity for mischief.

"How can I fight the Lilliputians in my organization?"

Start at the beginning of the pipeline:

1. Ask every prospective candidate where he fit on his previous company's organizational chart. Make him draw the chart, point

out the authority he wielded, the people he supervised, the money he managed, and so forth.

2. Ask him to describe how he put his job on the line, what suggestions he recommended that management adopted. What were the results?

3. Process all this raw material in your reference checkout.

4. Always ask what his *line* contribution was to an employer; not so much his *staff* work, as his *operational* effectiveness. Make him give examples of where he was *out front*. The key word is *accountability:* when, where, what, and how?

Straight answers to these questions reveal either a latent shelf-sitter or a potential self-starter.

"Technicians?"

"Always on tap—never on top."

PR men, lawyers, headhunters, accountants, engineers, writers—the list is endless. Keep the experts on the shelf and refer to them, like a dictionary, when you can't figure out how to spell your problem.

"Where I work the whole organization is nothing but a conglomerate of specialists."

So are most places of work these days.

War is too important to be left to the generals.

Education is too important to be left to educators.

The economy is too important to be left to businessmen.

A mark of a really growing organization is the combustible mixture of every race, creed, color, nationality, specialty—thinkers and doers —age grouping, I.Q., all harnessed to a common objective. In my ideal world:

- Dr. Spock is a consultant to the Secretary of Defense.
- Ralph Nader is an honorary chairman of General Motors.
- "Scoop" Jackson is a frequent consultant to the Arms Control Agency.
- Senator Proxmire consults to the Shell Oil president.
- The NAM president guest lectures at the Association of Radical Economists.

And in organizations where you work, where conflict is fostered, where compromise is discouraged, where conviction is inspired— where every workday there are winners and losers and every flower blooms—all of us are having so much fun we forget it's Friday and can't wait 'til Monday.

Wildly unrealistic?

I'm not so sure. Who can survey the past ten years in American history and gainsay that we are light-years closer to this ideal than in 1964? At one and the same time the United States is both the most established and the most revolutionary of societies. The reason the U.S.A. is the most interesting country on the globe.

"Basket cases"

Basket cases always have patrons. They phone to say, "Say, Dick, I wonder if you would mind talking to a guy who really needs help. I mean, he needs a job. Seems that he was teaching at Goddard and—to prove a point in his sociology class—mooned his students. Trouble is, the whole story is following him around the country, and he can't find a teaching job."

Or:

"Dick, there's this gal—knew her back in college. Managed a goat's milk co-operative in Venezuela for ten years and wants to break into investment banking. Can you help?"

Or:

"Now, it's true, Dick, this guy was fired from his last three jobs, but believe me, he's one helluva fine fellow and needs a job he can get his teeth into, someplace where he can make a difference."

Or:

"Well, true, she was into drugs—even horse—but I'm convinced that Barbara is getting her head together, now that her former husband has the kids and she's settled into a women's commune. Don't be put off by the tear-gas pistol she carries. . . ."

As an employer, don't waste your time hiring people whose personal lives are in ruins. Don't make their problems yours. Hiring someone because he *needs* a job is as bad as *not* firing someone who needs his. False compassion.

"What about people who project an institutional image?"

Every key player in your organization.

But some people are more "out front" than others.

The public information officer: a nice individual who tells lies for the good of his organization. The flakcatcher who is the "high corporate source" quoted by newsmen and is often an ex-media type himself. Well-paid, he doesn't understand the objectives or the operations of the place. This is why he is such an effective liar.

As the least-informed person in the organization and the last body in the shop who learns how a policy was arrived at, the good flakcatcher is winningly loyal to his employers, has a taste for being out front in the public eye, is a bear for punishment, and likes being called a member in good standing of the Establishment.

Flakcatchers have the mien and disposition of a chronic constipate. They would fit well in a newspaper's editorial department. They are wont to think that our country pays for its liberty with altogether too much license. Known to wear flag decals in their lapels.

Am I being too rough on PI people? Yes I am.

It's tough finding effective flakcatchers. The best should want to be an organic part of Top Management. They want to enunciate policy and help make it.

If you work for an honest organization, the flakcatcher is automatically a member of Top Management. If you work for a dishonest organization and are a flakcatcher, the chances are good that you work on the second floor of the place behind a frosted-glass window.

"Any special kinds of special assistants?"

Bag and ticket men.

Far better-paid than a valet, smarter than an airline attendant, and harder-working than the boss's domestic help, the good bag and ticket man is the soul of confidentiality. His chief qualification is that he never talks to anyone but the boss. His relationships with everyone else are guarded. His manner implies that he knows things of such import he simply must refuse the second scotch and soda you would eagerly pour for him. His job is to ease the boss through all of life's little sticky wickets: haircuts, airline tickets, a birthday present for the wife, and other obligations important lives are heir to.

The bag and ticket man travels everywhere with the boss and is sometimes a guest on Christmas day at the family manse. Nobody is sure why, but the bag and ticket man is always a man, always single, and always under thirty. Sometimes he is a distant family relative or friend. The bag and ticket man works closely with the boss's special assistants, especially the confidential secretary. His salary is not widely known. His humor is restricted to laughing at the boss's jokes. The soul of discretion, he knows how to leaven his power with tact. The worst thing that can happen to him is to make his boss late for an airplane or lose the boss's bags en route.

"How do you pick special assistants?"

If you are anything like some CEOs, a sure sign of managerial *hubris* is the character of your special assistants.

The effective monarch delegates his authority to dukes and barons of the realm: the operational people.

But King Richard is piggish, keeps power to himself, locks his women in chastity belts, hires food tasters and court jesters, and makes high policy in the Star Chamber surrounded by sycophants.

Medievalism overtakes you when you think you are so important ("after all, I'm so great I earn seventy-five thousand dollars—I'd better make all the decisions") to an organization that you must call the plays from the sidelines. You hire a bevy of "assistants-to," all of whom use the power you won't give up, to undermine or "control" the work of their betters who have the responsibility two steps down the organizational chart.

If your work is so important you *can't* delegate it, be sure your special assistants are (1) rotated frequently, (2) compensated far less than your operating chiefs, and (3) understand that they are conduits to the Power House and not the Main Switch.

Infantry officers in the front trenches *loathe* light colonels warm and safe behind the front lines at headquarters banging the general's ear. Under no circumstances must special assistants act in the name of the boss without explicit authority to do so. The *responsible* authority in any kind of organization is never wielded by satellites of the sun. Responsible authority is the province of the CEO and his departmental chiefs, the King and his noblemen.

Great special assistants *never* try to protect the boss. Their job is to be bearers of bad news.

Special assistants are never photographed, nor the subject of gossip, hardly on a first-name basis with more than five people, and act with circumspection, dispatch, prudence, and good sense.

Behind every great man or woman there are special assistants whose greatness is their anonymity, who the nobles of the realm remember with esteem and affection because these persons made their jobs easier.

"Assistants-to" should be gatekeepers, not toll collectors.

"What do you mean by the term 'gatekeepers'?"

Often called special assistants, confidential secretaries, administrative aides, palace guards.

They control access: access to the boss, to power, to information, to the decision-making process.

Gatekeepers surround the boss, screen his phone calls, read his mail, write his letters, develop his agendas, compose his speeches, and control information he needs to make a decision. Gatekeeper jobs are as important as the boss's, which is why they are so eagerly sought.

Refer to the Watergate testimony of Ehrlichman, Haldeman, Higby—gatekeepers par excellence, who became *de facto* authority in the U.S.A. That's why when the boss is cashiered or retires, his special assistants leave to be replaced by a whole swatch of new *outsiders*. One of the qualifications of a good gatekeeper is to be an outsider.

"You say somewhere that a mark of a growing organization is the mixture of thinkers and doers. How do you find the thinkers?"

Eggheads.

Lawyers, economists, analysts, evaluators, Ph.D. physicians.

"Does he have analytical smarts?" Which is the question my boss asks when we bring eggheads on board. Can this person think *straight, propositionally, logically,* or is he a fuzzy-wuzzy.

Can the candidate break down a problem, reassemble it, and *explain* why something works? The analytical capability, as rare as a rainy day in June, is appraised in a candidate's *writing* samples. If what you read is mumbo jumbo, another Ph.D. exercise of the obvious or ill-thought-out and badly organized—no matter how profound the subject, buyer beware.

Intellectual quackery in the marketplace is endemic these days. Never hire an egghead on the bases of degrees, education, and/or even recommendations—eggheads, like medical doctors, never knock each other outside trade circles. A conspiracy of silence follows eggheads from job to job.

So in hiring for the "analytical capability," (1) see as many applicants as possible, (2) set up functional interviews for the candidate with experts you trust, (3) couch questions that tax a candidate's ability to *think,* (4) do a close textual analysis of his writings, and (5) do an exhaustive reference checkout.

And never hire anyone who uses—with a straight face—adjectives like "holistic" or "heuristic"!

"How do you select a marketing man?"

Simple.

First: Can he sell himself? That's why all savvy job seekers are marketing types.

Second: Can he be sold? A test of a good salesman is his own capacity to buy products, services, people, and ideas. An effective salesman always admires another person's sales effort; he's a good "mooch" himself. Salesmen like to watch another salesman "pitch."

Good salesmen represent any kind of personality: shy or social, outgoing or introspective, aggressive or timid (the most prosperous insurance agent I've known was as timid as a titmouse). There are as many *kinds* of effective salesmen as there are kinds of personalities.

Other qualities to search out: Salesmen know how to be *rejected;* they don't slash their wrists and bleed all over you when they blow a sale. Second, salesmen are not aggressive—they are persistent; they never give up *if* they believe what they are selling *helps* a customer. Third, effective salesmen are *trustworthy:* People *trust* them. Trust is the essence, remember, of the business relationship.

Effective sales people are, like everyone else, hard to find. In business, they are shock troops on the front lines deserving your firm's highest medals of honor. Without those salesmen out front selling what you do, everyone where you work is unemployed.

"Secretaries?"

Impossible.

In ten years, I've found (and hired, which is to say stealthily wooed) nine crackerjack secretaries. Of about five hundred interviewed. My advice to your organization is to farm out the secretarial function, find secretarial consultants (people paid by the hour), or make any secretary you hire part of the first team; pay a lot of money for a good secretary. Recruit, you sexist beast, *male* applicants, graduates of the armed forces administrative schools, grad students with dancing fingers, immigrants fresh to our shores who hit that keyboard. Anyone who *wants* and *can do* the job is qualified. But how many people *want* to be secretaries any more?

Effective secretaries are, in fact, *the* organization—they make the place hum. Theirs are judgment jobs, no matter what the women's liberation movement proclaims.

"What about 'The Beautiful People'?"

They ski at St. Moritz, swim at St. Tropez, and summer in San Sebastian. They've met the Aga Khan, supped with Princess Grace, and call Leonard Bernstein, "Lennie." Fun to look at, they are hateful to work *with,* unless you need a cruise director, a nonworking board member, or a fund-raiser for the Symbionese Liberation Army.

Incompetent. Protected from life's little surprises by batteries of lawyers, caterers, doctors, accountants, tutors, tennis coaches, and travel agents, they have little stomach for important work. That's why they hire out surrogates, specialists, and other third parties to negotiate them through life's sticky wickets.

"If managing change is so important in organizational development, who are the people who can shake the place up?"

Corporate gunners.

They do the downfield blocking while corporate superstars carry the ball; they gadfly policy-makers; they practice guerrilla warfare on people not pulling their oars; they generally know how to make the right enemies.

Gunners are accomplished at reminding Top Management of its

real objectives. They are sometimes brilliant, always feisty, frequently wrong, and, when the organization is moving full speed ahead in the right direction, bored to tears. No manager can afford more than two or three gunners per hundred people; otherwise the place will shake to pieces. But institutions without their in-house range riders are never any fun.

"How about consultants?"

Consultants. One-man bands. Business healers.

The best work alone. Their fees, while high, nowhere equal what it costs to bring ADL to your company. And besides, one-man bands don't have to answer to a lot of porked-up pardners back at headquarters who spend their time thinking about profit maximization and forgetting client needs.

Check them out, like you would any other key officer in your firm.

No need to retain them. The best won't want, need, or recommend this kind of self-serving dependency relationship. What you do is pay them very, very well; good advice is the rarest of commodities and can save your firm millions of greenbacks, which you would otherwise incontinently spend on elaborate management studies, reorganization plans, wage and compensation programs—the heavy artillery of corporate administration, which chokes profits and defeats the spirit of your best people.

Here are some thoughts on consultants:

1. Most consultant services are too expensive; organizations that call on Booz, Allen and Hamilton are firms *that can afford the fee.* Therefore, managers hire consultants consonant with Parkinson's law, which says, *expenses rise to meet income.*

2. Every idea a management consultant shares with his client, which he mostly pulls out of the boiler plate back at headquarters, has been thought of by some sharpie deep in the bowels of your organization. The idea, however, never reached your level because communications in your organization are so bad (which is to say that people confrontations are cleverly discouraged by elaborate administrative procedure) that no one with clout can transform the idea through from conceptualization to implementation. Moreover, organizational stability is not served adopting ideas percolated within your organization because politically one department steals a march on another.

Just what an organization wants, isn't it?

Unhappily, it isn't. Many managers like to keep their people docile, dull, and safe; most prefer spending thousands of precious overhead dollars rather than act on their own people's advice. "Cresap, McCormack, & Padget's people told us this is what we gotta do and we paid them $175,000 for the advice and, by God, we're going to do it."

3. Never hire by brand names. So who cares that your agency has the bucks to hire McKinsey? The point is, if you really must spend money (so you don't have to give it back to the taxpayers or the shareholders or whomever you should give it to), insist that every consultancy job is done by an individual—not a firm. In hiring Big Ten consultancy firms, make sure you know *who* is going to do the work; check them out as *individuals*. Many big-league consultancy firms send their heavyweights in to lock up the business and are curiously absent when the work is being done. What your firm doesn't need is a lot of callow adolescents straight from the better business schools making 'twixt fifteen thousand dollars and thirty thousand dollars per annum while your company is billed at the rate of five hundred per day.

4. A bad management consultant is as worthless as the *size, weight,* and *slickness* quotient of his final report. The best advice is verbal, trenchant, given with conviction, and can be understood by the brightest mailroom attendant. That's why the best consultants, the ones who really know their business, only need a day or two to give you the advice you need. Their "data base" is in their head; no need for PERT programming techniques, flow charts, and bar graphs, a fancily bound leather binding containing an incorrigibly dull, pedantic text.

5. Good consultants give you their home phone number and are on the spot when you need them. Above all, they talk in plain Anglo-Saxon and eschew the usual business-school jargon.

6. Finally, and most important, a good management consultant *cares.* He is not competing against anyone except himself; he makes so much money he has time to do what he *wants;* he can look at your problem objectively; he genuinely *likes* you, although he often thinks your head needs shrinking, and he tells *painful and disturbing* things about yourself and your organization. The rare, great consultant is probably one of three people in America most effective chief executive officers feel truly comfortable with . . . all the time. Good man-

agement consultants, like rare vintage wines, are hard to find, terribly expensive, are sparingly used, and are always blessedly antibureaucratic.

"Any special characteristics to watch for in a good finance man?"

Finance is not my department, as my boss would be eager to tell you. But I can spot a good man with sums a thousand paces off in a blinding snowstorm. In most organizations he is the company comptroller—the chap who knows above all else that cash in must exceed cash out. As such, the comptroller is a royal pain in the ass to those in programming, production, R&D, and marketing.

As one who employs a good many people, you work closely with the comptroller. A good argument can be made that the comptroller is the "personnel" man. It is this important individual who determines whether you can afford to fill a job in the first place. "Direct costs" are the costs to the company for the salaries it pays, the most important part of any organizational budget. Reduce "direct costs" and organizations become solvent. That's the job of the comptroller.

Characteristics of a good finance man?

First, he betrays the traits similar to those of a good banker: prudence and sobriety. Who, in heaven's name, wants his banker to be a jolly old elf with a hankering for wine, women, and song? Not me or you. Finance people should remind you of your maiden aunt. They should be conservative in everything but politics, question every expenditure, and gadfly those who regard company funds as funny money infinitely available.

Facts.

That's what a finance man craves. Dreams, endeavors, and grand aspirations are for him anathema. A deep concern for solvency, a strong suspicion of those who spend money he accounts for, a finance person's real forte is to ruthlessly critique organizational methods and objectives.

"Is an effective finance person a candidate to be the CEO?"

Oh, yes, indeed.

To do so, however, he must make one helluva transvaluation in his personality, temperament, and drinking habits. After all, organizations do have purposes: They exist, it is thought, to *do* something. Finance people, thus, are well advised to learn how, in fact, money is earned. Otherwise, they remain fundamentally accountants—good men for double-entry bookkeeping problems, but the wrong man at the wrong time with the wrong qualities for leadership.

"Does business need to find people with the entrepreneurial imagination?"

Not big business.

We are told by business-school intellectuals that the age of entrepreneurship is dead; ours is a century of "management." Those who *found* enterprises are not necessarily those who manage them. And, of course, the academics muster a good deal of supporting evidence to back up this proposition.

Free-wheeling spirits, many of them second-generation Americans, by the way, are deeply into the American ethos. And industry should protect this evanescent breed. The unhappy fact is that the entrepreneurial imagination is nowhere near as sought-after—particularly in large organizations—as it should be. Entrepreneurs innovate, open new markets, improve products, and inaugurate new systems.

Yes, it is easily identified; but rarely a "qualification" any more for jobs in large organizations. That's why real entrepreneurs usually "do their own thing," which is another subject.

"What about 'big company' vs. 'small company' people?"

A real difference.

If I were hiring for a big firm, I would stay away from people whose experience has been with small institutions. And vice versa.

Again, the scale problem rears its ugly head.

Big companies offer:

- wildly differentiated and sophisticated work assignments.
- fat budgets and a consequent "funny money" orientation.
- unheard-of job security.
- management problems and opportunities different in *kind* rather than degree from small-company counterparts.

Small firms:

- know the value of a dollar.
- rarely offer total job security.
- are extremely limited in tasks, assignments, and places of work.
- rarely worship the personnel process.
- are more fun.

There are many more differences. My point: Scan every job applicant's work background and probe to find out whether your environment is congenial to his work style.

"Is there such a thing as a 'company man'?"

I meet them in airplanes, bars, and spot them quickly in job interviews. "The company has been good to me," is how they give themselves away.

I greet this comment with the stony stare of a man about to hang up on a telephone solicitor. "The company has been good to me" theme is the recurrent melody I hear in a lot of on-the-job situations, all of which makes Ravel's "Bolero" sound like a rock hymn. The statement rings with all the sincerity of a cemetery salesman about to score on an old people's home.

No, bless our hearts, we are all company men. But the company that suffocates you with fringe benefits, guarantees lifelong employment, and bastes you in corporate benignity *is not good*. It's like choking on your fourth glass of eggnog.

What company men should want is a challenging job. "The company has been good to me" means they don't. Translated from the Chinese, the company man is saying, "Help! I want my gonads back!"

"Is there any truth in the adage that people can transit from commercial into nonprofit jobs but never vice versa?"

Like the big company vs. small company situation, anthropological problems surface. A person who raises money for Common Cause, say, might be a bust as a marketing man for Warner-Lambert. Working environments, goals, and tone of institutions acclimatize people. Institutions, again, radiate personality, values, priorities; we are easily inured to certain kinds of institutions—commercial, nonprofit, academic, governmental, military.

In picking people, never wholly exclude candidates drawn from diverse fields (many will be the *best* candidates you find), but subject these candidates to a series of courtesy interviews throughout your firm to see how they like the tone of the place and how the place likes them. In the trade, these are called "information" interviews—two parties to a potential transaction swapping information about each other.

"How about choosing technical people for growth jobs?"

Writers. Statisticians. Questionnaire designers. Computer programmers. Social scientists. Market researchers. Photographers. Designers. Et al.

Again, use the functional approach: (1) Hire someone who is tops in the field; subject any candidates to their "trade" evaluation. (2) "By their fruits you shall know them"—study a writer's writing, a designer's designs, a photographer's photographs, a speechwriter's speeches, and so forth.

Specialists never go on a job search without a portfolio of their work. Judge its quality, be the supercritic. Everything else—education, experience, hobbies, personal characteristics—are utterly tangential. Stick to the flair factors: work accomplished and in hand.

"Well, writing samples are important for almost any judgment job, right?"

My boss calls writers "scribblers" or "blue-pencil bluenoses."
Wordsmithies.

For most judgment jobs, writing skill is a *sine qua non*. In government, especially. But there are different kinds of writing: descriptive, analytical, reportorial, social scientific, technical. If someone tells you he's a writer, ask him what *kind*. Then ask for samples.

Writers, like artists, are not necessarily doers. Often they prefer researching a problem, not *acting* on it: observers, not participants. Never hire a writer, as such, for an action job where decisiveness (acting necessarily on insufficient and unavailable information) and speed are important—unless the candidate's other flair factors mesh against the job.

So, in hiring writers, like everyone else, ask yourself what the essence of the job is. Plenty of people who can't write, *can* act. Don't let anyone "write" himself into a job where other flair factors are required.

CHAPTER 9

People, not personnel

"What do you mean?"

The people function is the foremost weapon in management's arsenal, exceeding even financial planning, marketing, quality control, R&D, and policy analysis. Top Management spends a good deal of time worrying about productivity, higher earnings, greater sales, and a better product. The time is better spent on the care and cultivation of those who make the qualitative difference between success and failure: the people who make it all happen.

First, eliminate the office, titles, budgets, and powers of the personnel people and widely disperse them throughout your organization. Don't apologize, since personnel's absence will hardly be noticed. Second, destroy all personnel manuals. Throw away salary schedules, personnel memoranda on dress, hours of work, work standards, uniform behavior codes, and all the rest.

Amalgamate your personnel people into various divisions. Let them learn the trade practiced in each division. If marketing, let them sell; if finance, let them handle accounts receivable; if purchasing, let them contact suppliers. In a word, let them absorb a trade, gain an expertise in an important part of the company. Once this on-the-job training has elapsed for six months, reassemble and appoint them as assistant vice presidents to the manpower manager.

Thenceforward, the manpower people become an organizational fifth column, an intelligence system loyal to headquarters but responsible to separate division chiefs.

A tricky political situation, you observe.

But that's what people experts are good at: to broker, middleman, go-between *other* people.

If they can't, then they have no business being in the people business. Their jobs are similar to diplomats paid by one government and accredited to another, consultants who serve their company and their client at the same time, or labor mediators responsible to both management and the union.

Third, Top Management makes sure that manpower people understand their main mission: finding, helping, and exiting people. The spigot of jobs is turned on at one end; at the other, the plug is pulled. How long people last in the pipeline depends on how much they have their eye on the organizational ball. If it slips, down the tube they go, gurgle . . . glug. Manpower people need to remind themselves that they might be the next to go.

Fourth, manpower people become "transition employment specialists" (which will please them—it's another title they can add to their own résumés), who are to be the employment counselors to everyone in the shop—from the boss on down. Helping people think through who it is they are, what it is they are doing at ABC, Inc., is a vital task in your organization.

"Won't reporting to two different superiors—a manpower vice president and a division chief—foul up lines of authority?"

Plenty of people have more than one "boss" where they work. In the collegial work environment of the '70s where the "task" orientation toward work is encouraged it is not unusual to have more than two people you report to.

Dispersing personnel people throughout your organization's divisions assures Top Management of close communication on "people" matters and at the same time formalizes each division's relative autonomy. This approach has particular merit in fostering recruiting programs aimed at the hiring of minorities. Moreover, it isolates the recruitment function within individual departments, all of which corresponds to the real power centers within organizations.

My quarrel with having a personnel division is that this department has no real clout. Every savvy job seeker knows never to look for a job in personnel. Why not structure an organization to take this elementary fact into account?

Sure, plenty of personnel types are going to fight this tooth and nail. But such a plan is in every personnel person's self-interest. Established in a "real" department with authentic hiring/firing power, "personnel" people will finally have some power of their own and focus on the primary aim of sound personnel policy: the hiring of the best people available. Such a plan will attract an altogether different breed of people into personnel work.

"How can manpower people help those people who are fired?"

A boon to most suddenly separated executives, since manpower people are specialists in transiting executives from one field to another. Such people render invaluable supportive service when an ex-executive needs it most. Manpower people can prevent a newly fired man or woman from making rash mistakes—when the gorge is still rising. And help him think through the next chapter in his occupational life.

Such a service shows that organizations *do* care about people they must let go. Organizations *should,* since they share 50 per cent of the responsibility for someone not working out on the job.

Such out-placement facilities are a crucially important part of every institution's people systems.

Moreover, who is to say, stranger things have happened, that someone newly fired might be rehired another day, once corporate winds are blowing in another direction?

Good people are hard to find. Keeping the newly fired as friends and as possible resource consultants is the way organizations invest a large deposit in the institution's memory bank. And people you let go are often potential customers of your organization's services. After all, they know your firm and what it can do more than anyone else.

"What kind of success have you had in recycling people from one field to another?"

I tried to persuade a university to hire an ex-diplomat to teach modern diplomatic practices. "But he has no Ph.D.," was the reply.

An ex-military man was, I thought, perfect for the job of heading a large organization's truck fleet. "But we need men with at least five years' experience in the industry," said my client.

But my success rate is heartening, too.

I've brokered ex-Catholic priests into high-pressure social action jobs, a woman with an eye for figures and no accounting degree into an unusual kind of cost accounting job, a bureaucrat into a trade school principal's job.

All of these placements worked out.

Examples of finding good people in the funniest places abound. Why not a conscious effort on your part—where you work—to encourage offbeat and unusual candidates?

"How important are the exit interviews?"

Very.

In an exit interview you find out how management "failed." You want to learn from your department's mistakes, and your exit interviews should reveal a wealth of information about leadership styles. It's a good time, as well, to let the people you're letting go know what specifically they did or didn't do. Of course, the whole business might have been unnecessary if you had taken the initiative before your best people needed to quit or had to be fired, which is why many divorced people begin to communicate *after* they have decided to break the tie. Not exactly the best matrimonial or employment strategy.

Manpower people should establish some fairly elementary exit procedures:

(1) Let any executive who goes to the guillotine keep his office, title, and secretary for a three-month period.

(2) Let him receive and make phone calls.

(3) Establish his severance pay on a monthly allotment scheme so he can finance a new job search.

(4) Let him have a verbal summary of why he was fired so he can base his story with his next employer on the real facts.

"Do you think Top Management will give up the personnel department?"

In growth organizations, yes.

For institutions on the downward slope of a curve, no.

Knowing how to use power means knowing how to give it up. Top Management, secure that its organization is pursuing the right objectives, feels free to increase efficiency among the hired hands by dispersing power to hire on a departmental, task-oriented basis. That means that Top Management keeps hands off all hiring decisions except in the executive secretariat, and hiring barons of the realm.

The savings in paperwork, downtime, and money are transparent. And isn't Top Management interested in making/saving money?

"How can you tell when organizations are on the downward slope of a bell curve?"

The Roman Empire began its decline in the first century A.D.
General Motors, in the early fifties.
The Federal Trade Commission, in 1952.
Life magazine, in the midfifties.

The sure sign of decline is an organizational loss of nerve, not coming to grips with new problems; managers exist to serve themselves—not customers, students, target populations.

There are three ways to face organizational problems: (1) Let the situation grow worse. (2) Circumvent the problem, go around it, and invent new institutions to manage it (the nonjob is a product of circumvential problem-solving). (3) Face the problem head-on and try to manage it, reduce it, and eventually eliminate it (causing, of course, more problems!).

A sure sign of decline is the cancerous growth in bureaucracies due to the inability to fire people.

"What about using computers to help the recruiting function?"

The computer crapout.

Swell, when it performs the accounting function—payrolls, for example. A royal pain in the *derrière* otherwise. Paper, paper, everywhere.

Why all this busywork? Why all these half-assed manpower disposition reports? For whom? To what end? Let your best systems people cost-out the expense of keeping up-to-date records and the outcome, sure as the north wind brings cold air is much ado about nothing equals naught. And it's expensive.

The EDP revolution and its impact on the "personnel process" has unquestionably augmented overhead costs and invited invasions of personal privacy. What's worse is that recruitment strategies are now being built around an EDP capability. Horrendously expensive and completely impractical. The triumph of technology over common sense.

"Why, what we'll do is program all these radiologists on tape and pull from the talent bank when we need the right man for the job," says the expert.

It doesn't work because there are not enough key punch operators to record, update, delete, and generally transform information about people.

Remember, people and their objectives are changing all the time!

That's why you throw away every résumé after it's six months old. People are changing: They marry, divorce, die, take new jobs, go back to school, join movements, get sick, leave the country, go to Washington, inherit money. All of which makes their objectives different. And no computer is smart enough to record the hidden agendas lurking in everyone's heart.

So when the Honeywell salesmen show up with fancy hardware to gull Top Management into buying flashy toys to manage manpower problems, scream, "It's a holdup!"

This advice is worth millions of dollars.

Don't let your organization fall on its knees to worship the personnel process.

Americans have a terrible propensity to throw money and hardware at human problems. The teaching machine replaces the teacher, firepower takes the footslogger's place, Dial-a-Prayer, Music-by-Muzak, 3-D porn movies, computerized salary negotiations, and the mechanically graded multiple choice test are a piece of the same cloth: the progressive downward spiral of civilization, the mechanization of culture, a loss of nerve.

"What about companywide policies forbidding (or encouraging) the hiring of relatives?"

There are companies that only hire blood relatives, sometimes extended families, and function well.

There are other organizations that flatly refuse to hire anyone related by blood or marriage.

The consanguinity factor is one your company might have addressed. There might be a whole chapter in your operations manual on the Do's and Don'ts of hiring your kid brother as a messenger in the Distribution Department.

My advice is to ignore the business entirely—the fewer policies management contends with, the better the quality of employment, and the better-quality people.

Who says my wife can't work of a Saturday morning to put my notoriously bad filing system in order?

And why can't the boss hire his daughter as a short-term receptionist during her spring vacation?

And why can't this woman's lover be a consultant to your Production Department?

There is no end to it.

Establish a policy, make a rule, and presto, another irrelevancy to confound. Another triumph of administrative ignorance over common, everyday experience.

Every employment decision is individual. In some cases, the sentiment factor might be taken into account. But effective managers who put organizations first will gladly fire their wives (or their husbands), reprimand the meekest nephew, and box the ears of their eldest son *if they don't cut the mustard*. Ineffective people, whether they hire relatives or not, are going to hire third-rate people in all events. The point to address in firing a manager is not his favoring relatives on the payroll—but his hiring ineffective relatives!

"How important are job titles in attracting effective people?"

Human relationists think they are *very* important.

So much so that job titles conceal more than they reveal, cause institutionwide identity problems, and hobble effective communication. All in the name of stroking the ego.

Yesterday in America, we called people "clerks"; today they are "administrative technicians"; yesterday we called people "salesmen"; today they are "marketing engineers"; garbagemen have become "solid-waste technicians"; ticket takers are "ramp engineers"; and press agents are "public information specialists."

All are products of the industrial imagination. Note how many titles are pseudotechnical.

In addition to corrupting language, obscuring communication, and generally deluding postmodern man, playing games with phony job titles causes a good deal of the management manipulation younger people so rightly complain about.

A good test of whether you manage by the book or by the seat of your pants is whether you victimize your people with titles wholly inappropriate to what they do, or whether you call bread, *bread,* a whorehouse, a *whorehouse,* and a salesman, a *salesman.*

"What about the increased labor unionization of technical and specialized employees?"

IBM has the right answer.

Pay people *more* than the industrial wage scale. And keep white-collar trade unionism off the company grounds!

Why?

Trade union leadership discourages face-to-face negotiation between managers and the managed. It substitutes its own representation, which is exclusively concerned with maintenance and compensation factors, forgetting that productivity is the only real index of pay. Equality of wage scale is foremost in the minds of the professional trade unionist—no matter that performance among professionals is wildly different and depends on task, time, degree of difficulty, and resources available.

Professionals, technicians, and specialists who abdicate the right to bargain individually about productivity and pay, abdicate a basic freedom in the name of collective security. And managers and the managed don't meet head-on individually in a real confrontational situation. Score ten points for the drone bees; worker bees: zero. Another example of the degradation of the democratic dogma.

"Are growth jobs well paid?"

Yes . . . and no.

Peace Corps volunteers are paid nothing but subsistence; otherwise they would be ineffective.

The chairman of the Executive Committee at Procter & Gamble makes $425,000. Would he be any less effective if he were paid $25,000 per annum?

My point is simple: There is little correspondence between what we are paid and how effective/happy we are on the job.

This flies in the face of "executive compensation experts," replete in the institutional life of our country, who are hell-bent on overpaying the white-collar classes.

I'm with Bob Townsend and others who believe that no chief executive officer should be paid more than $30,000 straight salary. Everything else the CEO earns should be based on a percentage of profits—which could mean a helluva lot *more* than $425,000 per year!

Pay should be based on production. No, *not* effort, or good intentions, or past performance, or future expectations. "What have you done for me lately?" is a question every boss should ask the hired hands at the salary negotiation session.

No, money isn't the most important thing. But it can be the *second* most important thing if compensation is based on strict performance/productivity standards.

"Why can't there be an independent personnel ombudsman to review cases of compensatory inequity within organizations?"

There are a number of reasons:

1. Legislating salaries based on job assignment invites the trade union mentality into the executive suite.

2. It *centralizes* decision-making power in a "Personnel" Division, when this function should be widely dispersed throughout the company.

3. It establishes wholly irrelevant indices on which to base compensation: years in grade, number of people supervised, standing on the organizational chart, and so forth.

4. It ties the hands of your key people in dealing *individually* with the people they supervise.

5. It substitutes a *process* for personal confrontation between the managed and the managers.

The result is an organizational hardening of the arteries. Wage and salary programs, personnel *ombudsmen,* and grievance committees are all deadly placebos that humor people but that never grapple with the far more important issues of pay *and* productivity.

Whether five hundred people report to you or only one, yours is the right to *negotiate* personally everyone's salary down the line. In healthy organizations, Top Management delegates this authority to middle managers, which encourages the middle managers to keep their eye on productivity and budgetary factors. Constant attention to individual performance on the job, which is *real equity,* is far superior to plausible but impractical schemes to establish organizationwide wage uniformity. In the Soviet Union this principle is called Stakhanovism; in the United States it used to be called "a day's pay for a day's work."

"How about automatic promotions?"

About as sensible as our national welfare policy. Instead of paying people to work, we encourage people not to work.

The result: ballooning of the welfare rolls and the destruction of morale among the blue-collar working population.

Automatic promotions are a product of "human relations" ("let's not hurt anyone's feelings") or organizational development administration (a data processing clerk in Division A must be paid what an EDP clerk in Division B is paid), even though the missions, means, and results of both divisions are as different from each other as the Swiss confederacy from imperial France.

No, the damage done in the name of democratic human relations is what Santayana meant about the degradation of democracy: The passion for equality among peoples destroys their natural, human, and healthy desire to be *excellent* in what they do.

"But how about all those noncommercial jobs—teaching, welfare work, correctional work—on which it is next to impossible to assess performance?"

That's my point.

What if we paid welfare workers—not a straight salary—but a flat five hundred dollars for every "client" they successfully rehabilitate, find a job, and eliminate from the public dole?

What if we paid teachers, let's say, five hundred dollars for every second-grader who learns how to read at a third-grade level?

What if we paid a probation officer five hundred dollars for every ex-con who transits successfully back into society?

A lot of complications, you say?

"Variable problems in equity compensation depend on degree of difficulty within the work environment and the target population," as a wage and salary administrator might say.

But I think paying people in "people jobs" on the basis of what they *do* would revolutionize results, attract a whole different breed of self-reliants into social service livelihoods, and, heaven forfend, actually solve social problems.

Utopian this idea is not. It is so reactionary, so consistent with the free-enterprise rhetoric, and so relatively easy of administration that we can be sure it will be bitterly resisted by the social service guilds.

"How are salaries negotiated?"

A few facts:

1. Nobody knows what someone else is "worth." "Pay him what he's worth" is what my boss says. What does that *mean?*

2. What you pay your top man or woman automatically predetermines executive pay for *all* of your managers down the line.

3. Too much attention is paid to "what the other fellow makes." In other words, pay scales are subtle badges of rank; "I'm paid more than X. Therefore, I am better than X." All is subsumed under the expression "comparability."

4. Executive compensation is not rationally negotiated on the basis of productivity. Usually, prevailing industrial rates, previous earnings, and futuristic expectations—plus hard bargaining on both parties' part—determine a final pay scale.

5. Executive pay rates are negotiated more and more on the basis of equity, not on performance. You are paid *relative* to someone else. Again, another example of corporate benignity run amok. In elephantine organizations, increasingly, the problem of equity among "comparable" executives being what it is, the whole business is delegated to the computer science types. A machine reckons more executive pay rates than is commonly thought.

6. Organizations continue to believe that money is what makes their best executives run.

"Are you saying that recruitment should focus on the 'challenging' aspects of the job to be done?"

Absolutely central.

Not to focus on what is to be achieved, on the contribution the task member is going to make, robs the organization and the individual of his main motivation in any kind of growth job: accomplishment.

That's what we remember about any job that gave us satisfaction. And it's what we mean when we say to the boss, "I want to feel effective." If you want to turn your people on, find out what makes them turn on.

"I can't motivate you; you can't motivate me."

But I can motivate me; you can motivate you.

"You are surely not dismissing money as a factor in motivating people?"

No, indeed.

As a headhunter, however, I've discovered that money is not the foremost factor in what people want. Most effective people are well paid. Money is what follows outstanding performance.

My hunch is that people begin to make the money issue their chief complaint about a company when they are inherently dissatisfied with other aspects of their job. In other words, the usual complaints about being underpaid are another signal people send to management which means they want to quit or be fired.

At the same time, it's worth remembering—particularly in these inflationary times—that economic survival (which is a job objective of everybody) is increasingly difficult. Money (and more of it) can become a legitimate reason for working. That's why there are fewer ostensibly unhappy people on the job in recessionary times than during boom periods when good jobs are easy to find.

All of which leads up to my main point: elaborate and generous executive compensation schemes, based on trade and industrial averages, previous earnings, in-house executive compensation uniformity, and so forth, overlook the most important reason people go to work. And that reason is to perform effectively at a task people like to do.

"Yes, but don't employers compete for talent in the executive marketplace and pay to find the best people?"

Most employers do. But, remember, competing to find outstanding people isn't a case of outbidding a competitor's salary offer. Most complex judgment jobs are so different from one another that Firm A can outbid Firm B (even though the former can't pay what the latter can) because of the quality of the job offered. Moreover, if compensation is strictly based on productivity, Firm A will be deliriously happy about paying their all-star candidate twice as much as Firm B after a couple of years of outstanding productive performance.

"O.K., so people function best when they are challenged on the job. What about better working conditions, shorter hours?"

The maintenance factor.

Don't listen for a minute to people's complaints. Organizations have no obligation to improve working conditions today.

Managers constantly invent systems that *increase* dependency and defeat self-reliance. But self-reliant people are the secret of employee motivation.

Self-management moves people off their duffs.

"But you surely don't object to cost-of-living increments in the face of skyrocketing inflation?"

A terrible constant in our capitalistic, Western society: a built-in escalator that leads to infinity. It goes like this: The cost of living rose 10.8 per cent last year; therefore, at a minimum, everyone on the payroll, from the bank president to the safe deposit attendant, receives an automatic 10.8 per cent upward adjustment in pay. At the same time, managers are charged with increasing prices by the same amount. And another round of inflation begins.

No one knows how to break this vicious spiral any more than anyone knows how to put toothpaste back in the tube. Economists are helpless before the problem; the editorial boards of the media are silent. And the harried salaried classes run ever faster for fear of falling behind.

In your organization, naturally, cost-of-living increments, I betcha, are as usual and expected as the health and life insurance program.

I think they are dumsquat.

They only make sense if every employee and executive can prove to management's satisfaction that, in fact, each individual's productivity increased proportional to the cost of living. And where you work, insistence on this elementary fact is the way to hold down unwarranted pay raises, make all the hired hands more cost-conscious, and above all, compel managers to become productively cost-effective in the management of their people.

The trouble with cost-of-living increments is that they are not negotiable—they are automatic. But a pay raise is management's supreme arbitration tool; to let it lapse into a reflexive, computerized problem-solving situation is to abandon territory that an organization and its people should fight over. It should be incumbent on every jobholder to prove that he is 10.8 per cent, say, more productive than the year before; more knowledgeable about his work, more successful, and incrementally more effective. If a jobholder can't prove it (and studies on accurate objective and subjective indicators are a first responsibility of Top Management), then there should be—on management's part—a confrontational situation.

Is someone's productivity not keeping pace with the rise in the cost of living really worth retaining within the organization?

Doesn't it make more sense to hire someone else, at a lower price, with greater potential, thus cutting costs (an unheard-of phenomenon)? Isn't the best way, in a word, to make money *to stop losing it?*

"Won't this elimination of cost-of-living increments cause great employee turnover?"

And the answer is, "Of course!" If anything, there is not enough executive turnover in our country; people develop squatter's rights on jobs. Yearly productivity confrontations will make men out of your managers and provide the perfect forum for performance review.

No one has a right to an automatic raise just because the cost of living rises. The cost-of-living rise is augmented because wage and salary programs are tied to an impersonal mechanism like the cost-of-living index.

"Why is relating pay to productivity so important?"

Establishing productivity indices is relatively easy in industry, harder in government, and most difficult in social action/education and philanthropic enterprises—but not impossible anyplace; for there is nothing written anywhere that says you can't take into account nonobjective factors, such as company goodwill. The job of managers is to establish productivity indices consistent with mission goals and within the matrix and mandate of the larger organization. Before filling a job, therefore, managers must think through what these factors are.

Thinking a job through means developing the means to evaluate the performance of its occupant. If a university cannot measure the teaching performance of its faculty, a business the sales performance of its salesmen, or a management consulting firm the quality of its consultant's advice, then who is to know why X is a better teacher than Y, Z a better salesman than W, or S a superior management consultant to T. Better to pick and promote people by ouija board.

Productivity indices are central in evaluating work on a *task* basis.

"So the central problem is not what you pay people, but how you measure productivity on which you base pay?"

That's right. It's a difficult, complex, and a superimportant task—the supreme management problem (and opportunity). Matching every judgment jobholder and his individual productivity against clinically objective production standards.

Questions that need hard answers:

1. What is the *task?*
2. How much time will it take before results can be measured and performance evaluated?
3. How much money and how many people and outside resources does this *task* cost?
4. How important is *this task* compared to *that task* in meeting organizational objectives?

"Can't we understand productivity standards by referring to the job description?"

Job descriptions are hopeless, especially for judgment jobs.

Growth positions are quintessentially a series of "tasks" or assignments. Everyone in a growth job is on "special assignment." That's why there are no permanent jobs, why all work is on a "task force" basis, why everyone in a growth job is really growing.

"Well, isn't it simpler to base pay on the job title, grade, and level of the person in the organization?"

That's why nonjob holders are so outrageously overpaid.

No, again, it doesn't work.

Growth positions are too much in flux to commit to paper; managers are no more able to freeze people in neat little boxes with solid and dotted lines running every which way than they are able to "control" events.

The "task" definition of "work" obviates organizational charts as well as the need for job descriptions. To use either charts or job descriptions befouls managers in establishing "fair" compensation standards every time.

"What about the differentials in pay scales?"

Human-relations administrators hate conflict. And conflict must necessarily arise between manager and those managed. The conflict itself is an institutional necessity. It allows both parties to *negotiate* based on executive *productivity*. But hard bargaining between two human beings management avoids, not welcoming the messy, human business of personal confrontation.

Line managers should resist Top Management's impulse to control their right to evaluate, reward, and punish, based on executive productivity within the confines of the task force.

So who cares if a supervisor of data processing is paid more in financial analysis than his counterpart in R&D?

Top Management should welcome wild differentials in pay scales among its senior and middle managers as evidence that in every garden a thousand flowers bloom.

"Can you give some examples of how you pay people based on productivity?"

Here are three:

"My job for the next three months is to abstract every article written in the past ten years on population trends in Latin America. My staff includes three researchers, three writers, a demographer, and a secretary. Fifty thousand dollars is the limit of my spending authority. My report will be delivered no later than May 1. Progress reports will be verbal. If I finish by April 1, I receive a $1,500 bonus. If my work is so good as to generate add-on business for the firm, the organization and I will discuss a significant raise in base pay."

"I have one year to add $250,000 of new business in our West Coast operation. Spending limits are subject to negotiation with the West Coast regional manager, but in no case will it be less than $50,000. Staff, marketing strategy, and product lines are at my discretion. Should I add more than $250,000, I will receive a 5 per cent bonus of the difference between the first and the second figures. Should I not meet the quota, I will suffer a 10 per cent reduction in base salary, terminate the position, and negotiate reassignment, if any, within the firm."

"Of the sixteen students, three fourths will have been admitted into colleges by July 1. My staff includes four teachers, all of whom will be hired at my discretion. I have one year to complete the task. Should I meet my goal, I will be seriously considered for a promotion to that of 'senior teacher' with no less than a 20 per cent increase in pay. All texts, curricula, and tests are subject to review by the headmaster."

Simplistic?

I agree. But every salary negotiation should end up with something like these results.

"Should Top Management's expectations of women line managers be any different from that expected of men?"

Women as a *class* are no different from men. No more intuitive, sensitive, or able. When you say, where you work, "Women must be assertive to get ahead at ABC, Inc.," that's just as true for men.

Verily, having studied the sexes since I was thirteen years of age, I cannot think of a single differentiation on the job that holds up under logical analysis.

"Women will handle power far better than men," says the liberationist.

"Men are more analytical," says the sexist.

"Women are passive and less ambitious than men," says the traditionalist.

"Women are equal," says the suffragette.

All of those statements are false. No one is equal to anyone else; I can be more passive than my wife in a month of Sundays; intuition is no more a woman's forte than logic is a man's; women use and misuse power just like men.

So what's all the brouhaha about? Sure, men have to drop sexist bars to employment; but women must *want* the jobs they say they seek—let them general armies, manage corporations, run the subway trains, and clean out the Augean stables. Let women build institutions—whether they be nations or a string of boutiques. Let women seize the levers of power; organizations won't improve as a result, of course, but women will no longer be dependent on men for their living. Men will become freer to pursue what they want without the millstone of obligation ("I'd quit ABC, Inc., tomorrow if it weren't for the wife and kids") hanging like an amulet of slavery around their necks.

Now what, praise God, am I getting at . . . ? Well, in the world of work, as every place else, working with *other* people is to hazard emasculation. Again, on the job, employers—male and female, friends and colleagues, will try to *control* you, put you down subtly, habituate you to a pattern of occupational submission. Men are so accustomed to these dominance/submission patterns we have a hard time understanding women's strong feeling on the matter.

On the job, I have my feelings hurt every day and I bruise other people's sensitivities as well. I bleed some and make others bleed, too. I am both the oppressed and the oppressor every day I go to work. Now this kind of atmosphere is found everywhere. It's not going to disappear because the National Organization for Women disapproves.

But people who fight back against oppression and against any class of oppressors are no longer psychologically enslaved, as plenty of Movement women have found out. To submit to oppression on the job, however, be you either man or woman, *is to be charged with not being aggressive enough*. That's why fighting for your convictions is so important. Why conflict is so healthy. "Sure, I'd like to promote Jane into marketing, but, frankly, she doesn't strike me as aggressive enough to close on our sales prospects." That's when Jane must rise up, charge into the boss's office and *insist* she hit the road with the other manufacturer's reps.

"But don't you agree almost all of the country's managers are men?"

Facts are facts. But I don't agree *entirely* that men are responsible. That male hegemony has been a deliberate policy to *bar* women from Top Management is a glittering half truth.

Of course, the whole subject of women's *oppression* on the job is a mine field. Women expect male employers, like myself, to capitulate to their views or they charge us with being closet sexists. My instincts prompt me to repress the whole subject and think about safer matters like the prospects of worldwide famine, ecological self-destruction, or a thermonuclear exchange. Moreover, I have an unhealthy sympathy for the self-proclaimed oppressed, unmitigated by a malignant sense of consideration toward people who maintain I *enslave* them. So it's no good my saying I totally agree with the women's movement; I don't. Moreover, given the fire storm of real rage women feel about men on the job, it is well to remember that passionate discourse on any dispute varies in inverse proportion to what we know. And wouldn't everyone agree—women and men— that we need a lot more information on the sexes and how we interact before we crucify men on the cross of male chauvinism?

The commonest answer to the above question, the male employer doing the talking, is, "More women would be in Top Management at ABC, Inc., if they were only as *aggressive* as men." Another glittering half truth. The truth is most men are not aggressive enough. A women asked this question might reply, "Ninety per cent of Top Management are men because they deny access to women. Ergo, we are oppressed." But it's truer to say that men not only oppress women, but other men. In a word, on the job, people oppress people. All the time. And *responsibility* for oppression lies as much with the oppressed as with the oppressors.

"Well, why is it women are more submissive than men on the job?"

Most women but by no means all!

What women are increasingly doing is ridding themselves (and the Women's Movement has been a big help) of the notion that they must be submissive, dependent, and nonassertive on the job. Many women who want to make a habit of success on the job, however, are still altogether too passive. Why? Help, I'm in deep water and going down for the third time, but I do believe—please, madam, don't throw that pipe wrench—many women are more submissive on the job than most men because they think that if they act independently, men won't *like* them on or *off* the job.

Now, quite the contrary. Men, true, have been socialized to expect women to be helplessly dependent on male protection—both at home and work. So men like me have a lot to learn. But dependency, as we have seen, is the root of all resentment, and women—over the centuries—have exacted a high price from men for their dependent enslavement. Thanks to the evolving revolution between the sexes, men will come to welcome women's increasingly independent and assertive behavior which helps free them from an obnoxious and unnecessary sense of obligation and guilt.

"What about affirmative action requirements to hire more women, blacks, and older people?"

The problem of discrimination.

If someone said you were a discriminating person, would you cry "Foul!"?

Hardly. Discriminating persons are people who judge.

But when it comes to hiring situations, our well-known discriminatory faculties vanish, to be replaced by an ersatz liberalism.

A good many employment decisions, as well as management ones, are made on the basis of the giving party ("management") feeling guilty about the receiving party (the "employee"). And decisions of no matter what kind that are secretly inspired by a guilt complex are always wrong.

A black man or woman is promoted into a job because management feels guilty about its horrendously bad discriminatory hiring practices.

A woman is hired from outside to be a vice president for the same reason.

An aging friend of the firm's founder is put on the payroll because the friend can't seem to find a job.

A bad secretary is promoted because she is of Spanish-speaking heritage.

"Aren't you assuming that if you happen to be a member of a minority group you can't be as qualified as a white Anglo-Saxon male?"

Good gravy, no!

Ability, talent, flair is rare enough without ascribing it to any race, sex, nationality, and so forth. My point is that the hiring/firing decision should be based on individual effectiveness. Anyone who recruits otherwise is crackers. And that goes for thousands of traditional employers who still draw exclusively from the white Anglo-Saxon manpower pool.

And that's the big trouble with the old-boy network. Old boys recommend old boys. All the more reason to dip into unconventional sources of talent.

There is a shortage of effective people in this country for its toughest jobs.

To hire on a nonelitist basis is a false liberalism, the triumph of class over individuals, of existence over essence, of processes over people.

Anyone hired because that person is a woman, black, poor, old, or Spanish-speaking (except when these externals constitute the flair factor for a job) knows in his or her heart that he or she has been the victim of another kind of discrimination.

"Yeah, but these class-action suits are no joke—we require a Personnel Department to respond."

But why the Personnel Department, *which doesn't do the hiring?* The action is in your operating departments. For example:

- an airline firm is sued for having a poor minority hiring record.
- a statewide savings and loan association is sued for having no recruitment plan to hire blacks.
- a government agency is sued for having no women in supergrade positions.
- a lumber firm is sued for having a segregated sales staff.

The onus of the class action is not exclusively on the organization companywide. Rather, the blame really resides maybe in only one department. Ten to one, at the airline, charter sales, legal counsel, customer relations, and maintenance services are well integrated. It's pilot training where the company needs to put its recruitment bucks if it wants to avoid a class-action suit. And it's that department that needs to correct its hiring deficiencies.

At the savings and loan association, I wager that the tellers, operational staff, and janitorial department are highly integrated. Focus on the New Business Department and Real Estate Loans Department—that's where you won't find blacks.

Equal opportunity employment officer programs flop because the man or woman hired is always a member of a minority (that's the only job in the organization that *shouldn't* be held by a woman or a black or member of another oppressed group) and because the job is located in the Personnel Department, which has no clout companywide. Top Management should make each operating department answer for its sexist, racist employment patterns.

"So you don't think the quota system works?"

Quotas never work.

We are a nation of minorities. The white Anglo-Saxon Protestant is one of the chief minority groups in many cities in America today. The greatest step you can take toward social democracy is to encourage nonsociological thinking. Which itself is a result not of the melting-pot theory, but the recognition that America must be kept safe for diversity.

No, our country is not a melting pot, but an interesting Irish stew. And organizational hiring patterns are increasingly reflecting the mainstream of Americans. It is now time to cease and desist from treating individuals as abstractions, "the poor, the black, the brown, the female, and the oppressed"—all of which is the perfervid rhetorical product of liberal politicians hungry for high office. Time—in the seventies—to stand back and base employment decisions on individuals rather than on groups; time to stop categorical thinking and restore individual discrimination; time to treat people as persons.

"That's fine in theory, but don't you agree that Top Management must pressure people down the line to hire people from different backgrounds?"

We are on the horns of a dilemma.

If Top Management presses for minority hire, ask and it shall be received. There will be a lot of wild, ill-considered promotions, assignments, and employment decisions based on fulfilling statistically satisfactory norms promulgated by the federal government (which is interesting, since Uncle Sam is a bigot, too). On the other hand, without any pressure either from the feds or Top Management, most organizations will continue to reflect an Anglo-Saxon white male dominance.

Solution?

Again, I think the answer lies not with the oppressors but with the *oppressed*. Anyone who believes he has been discriminated against because of age, race, sex, and so forth has a tool at hand that seems to be working effectively today. That's a lawsuit. Organizations with deplorable sexist and racist personnel patterns are ripe for losing millions of dollars if they demonstrably implement policy exclusionary of blacks, women, Vietnam vets, and so forth.

Organizations are not in business to lose money. Individuals and groups representing individuals should focus on the lawsuit as the single best way to break the back of discrimination.

Establishing a quota system and enforcing it simply turns a racist policy inside out. It is government-sanctioned racism and sexism just the same. Righting a wrong with another wrong does not make a right. Hiring, promoting, and *not* firing people because of their race, age, sex, etc. is a crime, too. And a general policy of reparations toward biased groups is simple extortion. Its implementation is bad management practice and in the long run an abdication of leadership which follows a loss of nerve.

"Well, clearly racism and sexism are part of the marketplace, but isn't age discrimination where it's really at?"

Another area of active discrimination is age. Of course, it's against the law, but it is practiced—age bias—more than sex or race discrimination. "Don't send me any fifty-plus types with paunches" was what my boss (a liberated woman nearing fifty herself) once ordered me.

The chances are that you won't hire anyone your elder for a position immediately beneath you in your organization's chain of command.

The chances are that you won't accept a job working *for* someone your demonstrable junior in years.

The chances are that you are going to feel uncomfortable working for someone exactly your own age.

If so, then the best strategy is to screen candidates to fill jobs in a range you can generationally live with.

But watch out: You're an age bigot!

"Well, I don't like that!"

Good for you.

Ideally, some place deep in the American psyche there is the perfect occupational age. It is thirty-five years old. And sure as eighty million people rise Monday morning and go to work, age bias will touch them before the race is run.

In hiring "teams" of people, age difference can be a plus and a minus. Ideally, mixing up ages—like mixing up other externals—

can pay off. But in some places, remarkable age differences cause generational conflicts in values, work habits, and life styles. As an employer, you must consciously decide whether age *is* or *is not* a factor. If not, you should consciously, again, ask yourself whether a variety of different ages is a plus. If not, then age *is* a factor in your equation, and you'd best hire people in the same generational span.

The older one gets, the less age becomes a factor in peer bonding and the less the above obtains. The age factor is where the young are most rigid and where older people are more flexible. And if your organization is so lucky as to have leadership where age discrimination is actively fought and where management's subjective instinct is to go with ability whether "too young" or "too old," then you are well advised to remain and "grow" with such an advanced outfit.

"How can I make 'personnel' into people where I work?"

Stop what you are doing wrong.

1. Eliminate all job descriptions and organizational charts.

2. Recycle everyone in the Personnel Department into your firm's chief operating departments.

3. Ask anyone doing the hiring to do the firing—be sure it's the same person, the man or woman blessed by higher power to be the leader. The "people" function is widely decentralized and dispersed in your organization.

4. Reduce every job to a series of tasks that can be described in twenty-five words or less. Don't confuse the issue through wordy and peripheral experiential and educational gobbledygook.

5. Make everyone who hires check out whether it's a growth job: What is the *real challenge* of the job? Bad answers or no answer to that question are invitations to the dependents/passives to take over your task force, project, department, or organization. If the score is low, what's wrong with him or her as a leader?

6. Continually update the task definition of work. Make your people write their own task definitions; then you, the boss, rewrite them. Then confer, negotiate, and agree on a third and final version. Make the person you hire *do* it; then you do it. Negotiate. Repeat the exercise whenever either party *wants* it—this can happen three or four times a year.

7. Negotiate compensation based solely on productivity. Make the "risk takers" rich.

8. Stop trying to "manage" your people; stop trying to control them; stop, stop, stop trying to motivate them.

9. Start managing by subjectives. Forward!

CHAPTER 10

Management by subjectives

"What do you mean by 'management by subjectives'?"

Management by subjectives means leadership.
Get on your people's side.
Be a leader. And that means being able to fire people, to court unpopularity, knowing how to work alone, welcoming the buck being passed to you—in a word, someone dependent on his own inner resources, who measures his progress by internal standards and does not require daily strokes from his "superiors," compliments from his peers, and gratitude from "subordinates."
That's when people are glad to play "Follow the Leader."

"What do you mean by 'getting on your people's side'?"

Anybody who works for an organization, whether in the executive secretariat or in the steno pool, is on the *same* side if organizational goals are clear, leadership is effective, and people are "motivated." Adversary relationships such as labor vs. capital, the Editorial Department vs. business services, and Top Management vs. middle management, are nonissues.
Make conflict, which is a precondition to progress, a fixed feature in your organization. Conflict causes problems to surface and illuminates real organizational goals. Conflict clarifies organizational objectives, which causes a resolution. Somebody or some department or some idea triumphs. There are winners and losers at work every day—unless, of course, the issue is circumvented, a mark of an organization in decline.
"Getting on your people's side" means that leaders *care* about their people. And that means that constant attention is paid to what people want.

"But I thought you said managers can't motivate people."

I also said that people can motivate themselves.

All of you know about contact lenses. They vastly improve people's appearance and are relatively inexpensive. Yet millions who can afford them don't buy contact lenses. Why?

Because they lack the motivation. An oculist, an ophthalmologist, or a "motivational" expert can't possibly make you use contact lenses unless you damn well want them.

The same with motivation on the job. Managers can't motivate people to do something *they don't want to do*.

But managers can find out what people want to do. That's the managers' job. And that's leadership.

A good deal has been written about Vince Lombardi, the great football coach. A manager of men. Why?

What most people don't remember about Lombardi is that he quickly rid himself of any player, no matter how talented, who wasn't "motivated" by his style of leadership. No, you can't motivate people; but you can lead them. If someone doesn't like your leadership, then better for both of you to part company. Trying to "motivate" talented people is a matter of picking people in the first place who *like you, your objectives, and want what you want*.

Managing by subjectives means leading people who *like* your leadership style and welcome your goals. And helping people *who don't,* to exit from your department or organization into another department (within your organization) or elsewhere.

"So taking frequent risks with people—the bold approach in hiring and firing them—is managing by subjectives?"

Yes.

No business decision is irrevocable.

A sure sign of a good businessman is his propensity to cut his losses; the sure sign of an effective people manager is his ability to fire.

To try to "live with your mistake" causes bad vibes all around and circumvents rather than solves the problem. The employee in question who is too timid to confront his own problem is gradually demoralized. Of course, that's the object of management; don't fire him, let him unravel *slowly* and *quit*.

"Bob, we blew it . . . together. I shouldn't have hired you; you shouldn't have accepted. So let's work together at the company's expense to find you another job, whether in-house or at another firm. I'm told it shouldn't take more than three months—keep your phone and stay at your desk. But from now on your job is to find another position."

The kind of conversation too few people have with their boss after the ax falleth.

"That way, when I fire Jones I won't feel like a perfect cad."

Good organizational planning trains people *to take care of themselves;* it eschews the organizational dependency relationship and makes people take responsibilities for their own lives.

Good people *hate* being dependent. They crave involvment; they want to make a contribution.

Stop what you are doing.

No more stock options, annual increments in pay, cost-of-living escalator clauses, free box seats at the Ice Follies, and on and on and on.

Manage by subjectives; find out what challenges your people, and if you can't provide it, help them find it elsewhere. That is the security people want—what comes from within themselves.

Then you can junk all your "permanent" jobs and forget the terms of tenure.

"So that's how to motivate people?"

Yes; get on their side and let them motivate themselves.

What motivates people is clear—a sense of effectiveness. Your job is to make people focus on what they *want,* help them overcome the anxiety this information causes, and match up their real objectives, if any, with the organization. And if the matchup can't happen (and most times it won't), assist them in recycling into another job within your firm or elsewhere with self-esteem intact.

This kind of attention to a person's real agenda is a liberating experience for both individuals and institutions. Once the wraps are off and the lying stops, once a frank interchange of goals is set forth, both parties support each other—the individual because his own interests are being served by the organization, which cares enough to help him find a better job (if necessary), and the organization because freer, self-reliant, and more effective people are the result.

"So leadership means getting inside your people's head?"

Yes.
Find out what makes Sammy run.
What are his subjectives?
What are his goals?
What does Sammy want?

"How do I become that kind of a leader?"

Caring is important. And I don't mean corporate compassion, which evades and circumvents People Problems.

Caring about people means getting on their side and finding out what *they want.* Tough. As tough as freeing people to get on the organization's side. But genuinely caring about people predisposes them to reconsider their role in the organization, which is a start in getting them on the organization's side.

Once that process is set in motion, Step 2 is to discover what a person's sense of effectiveness is, what his *flair* qualities are, what achievements, accomplishments, contributions—call them what you may—support this sense of effectiveness.

"Why is it so difficult thinking through our sense of effectiveness?"

Terrifying. People think that everyone else is effective but secretly dismiss their own talent. No joke. That's why so much downright lying goes on in an interview, why résumés are pitiful profiles of people's talent, why choosing people is a hazardous occupation.

The reason people can't focus on personal and professional goals is that our whole lives are spent fulfilling obligatory objectives established by (1) parents, (2) school, (3) the Church, (4) the military, (5) our friends, and (6) our employers. Assuming *institutional* goals, doing a job of work because we *should,* always putting ourself *second* are habits inculcated at infancy.

"It sounds easy, but is it?"

No, it's uphill work figuring out what people want and where they are effective. Another problem is the anxiety this self-knowledge causes. Let's return to my original point about how terrified most people are of their sense of effectiveness, how knowing what you want and can do well is often immobilizing, paralytic.

It's much easier wanting what Dad wants, the U. S. Marine Corps orders, the Sunbeam Corporation says, and so forth. Putting organizational goals ahead of personal desires makes one's work, one's "duty."

Horsefeathers.

Forcing a human being to do something violates his deepest instincts toward personal freedom and self-expression. Most people entering the job market do what they "should" rather than pursue what they "want." The result is alienation and a lowering of the vital signs of life.

In working with hundreds of unhappy jobholders, the source of the dissatisfaction comes out in examples like this:

• The research assistant whose deepest wish is to be a *chanteuse*.
• The military man who wants to go into refugee relief work.
• The social worker who wants to make lots of money.
• The Ph.D. social scientist who wants to be a little-theater producer.
• The headhunter who wants to write books.

"O.K. How do you find out what people want to achieve on the job?"

Make people throw away their résumés.

Insist that they sit down for three hours in an empty office (especially no telephone) with nothing but a yellow legal pad and a felt-tip pencil.

Tell them they can't go to lunch until they list every accomplishment on or off the job since they were five years old.

Look that list over together and figure out what it "means."

What surfaces is a pattern of contribution and effectiveness, carefully concealed on the résumé, which has important meaning to both of you.

Some of the questions you now will be able to answer are:

1. Does he work well under pressure?
2. Does he like/dislike competition?
3. Does he compete best himself or others?
4. Does he require group/individual or self-recognition for a job well done?
5. Is he badge-happy or a real achiever?
6. Is he a good deadline worker?
7. Does he have entrepreneurial instincts?
8. Does he have managerial potential?
9. Would he rather please himself than other people?
10. Does he work best in large or in small organizations?
11. Is he a craftsman, a politician, an ideamonger, thing-oriented, or money-minded?

The list could go on for the length of this book.

What's important is that this is a self-knowledge exercise. And the only answers you want are to the questions, "Where is this guy effective?" "Does his effectiveness mesh against the flair factors required on the job?"

"Can you give some examples of these achievement lists?"

O.K.

Read over the following three lists.

Candidate No. 1	*Candidate No. 2*	*Candidate No. 3*
Finished term paper assignment in three days without sleep.	Conducted open-ended business survey for employer that was used as basis for new marketing campaign.	Failed every subject in prep school except art. Was cited as the outstanding art student in the history of the school.
Beat out three other more qualified applicants for a key job in ABC, Inc., programming division.	Developed most successful profit center within ABC, Inc., on my own initiative with no encouragement from top management.	Landed three industrial clients for my consultant services: leasing antique furniture to cash-rich firms.

Candidate No. 1	*Candidate No. 2*	*Candidate No. 3*
Nominated by board chairman to attend prestigious mid-career-level business course from among twenty candidates selected by Top Management.	Started own self-service laundry scheme in college and financed college education on profits.	At University of Nancy, where I learned French, I completed four years of work in three semesters.
Chosen by fraternity as the brother most likely to succeed.	Broke my own record as high jump champion at college.	Wrought first industrial sculpture ever displayed in Europe from Army surplus material.
Cited by commanding general, Eighth Army, for being "Soldier of the Month" four times in succession.	Refused invitation to turn pro in order to enter law school full-time.	Declined full professorship in Art History at college that flunked me out ten years before.
One of twenty young men selected by Junior Jaycees as "Future Leaders of Industry."	Refused Junior Jaycee offer to become member despite strong organizational pressure to "mix" in community.	Published original work of art criticism, which was critically well received, but which sold only two thousand copies.
Never missed a deadline in five years' work in R&D.	Packaged complicated shopping-center real-estate scheme over five-year period.	Initiated first consumer advisory program in American museum history.

Well, the lists go on and on. But we know enough about all three of these fellows to make a fairly accurate judgment about where they "fit." If you are looking for a museum director, candidate No. 3 is your man. Want someone to start up a new component in your industry? No. 2 seems to fit. A regional manager for your firm's western office? No. 1 looks like he fits the bill of fare.

Get the idea?

That's what I mean by "management by subjectives." Find out what makes someone tick and match it against your organization's needs. If there's no match, both of you are bound to agree. Then it's time to recycle someone you like very much but can't use any more into another firm, field, or "career."

"Is it really that simple?"

No, of course not.

In reality, these lists are much longer, contain information about people that doesn't match *your* needs entirely, and often reveal a complete mismatch between what a person does and what he *wants*.

Plenty of people agonize writing out such a list. Self-knowledge is agonizing!

"What do you learn most from these lists?"

I learn how people feel *effective*.

This sense of effectiveness is what "motivates" them; nothing else will.

"Does it always follow that someone will want a job because he or she is effective at it?"

No.

Plenty of people are effective at *this*, but would rather do *that*. This is another reason why employers should beware of people "qualified" for a job: They can do a job, but they don't want it.

The problem goes back again to what people "want." If they don't *know* what they want, people do what they qualify for. And that's why people feel they don't fulfill their *potential*—and why employers make so many mismatches.

"Isn't this technique just another device to motivate people?"

No, indeed!

Remember, managers can't motivate anyone except themselves. There is no way—not through industrial relations or sensitivity training or transcendental meditation—that your people are going to turn on to what you *want* them to do. Whether management dangles a carrot in front of its people or gives them a collective kick in the avoirdupois, no one is motivated except the manager.

Most job candidates *say* they are self-starters, but faced with a job where pay is based on productivity and self-reliance is encouraged, they quickly back off—another reason why a good man or woman is always hard to find.

"So overpaying Jones and making him more comfortable on the job isn't the answer?"

When what is wanted is making Jones feel challenged, tested, and fulfilled on the job. So instead of saying, "Thank God it's Friday," he says, "Golly, it's Monday!"

Job security, apparently the most sought-after characteristic in any kind of job—judgmental or otherwise—is a chimera of the mediocre classes and a pain in the *derrière* to the meritocracy. While no one, least of all your humble correspondent, doubts that the lust for personal security animates nearly every occupational move in our society, it is true that real security can only come from within. And the aim of people development is to create those working conditions that positively *test* a jobholder, that creates a manageable anxiety, which cause people to grow, to feel effective.

Work, remember, is an honorable estate. It is what we *want* to do, not what we *must*—which is labor.

To labor in order to feel secure against the slings and arrows of outrageous fortune violates our deepest want: freedom to express and fulfill ourselves.

Because the only real security is in oneself.

Make people believe they are their own security!

Encourage a high turnover in executive employment (that is, expect it and *plan* for it).

Train people to focus on their real talent, and assist in recycling them into progressively more responsible employment within or without your organization.

"It seems to me that every leader must become a psychoanalyst."

No manager—that is, no real leader—is going to hesitate, if he or she is interested in human motivation, in helping someone find out what that person wants. Wanting something, doing a job of work out of a sense of mission (rather than duty), working at a job (loving it) rather than laboring at it out of a sick sense of obligation (hating it), and as a result feeling effective on the job are the mainsprings of human motivation on the job.

That's why compensation and maintenance programs (salary, fringe benefits, and work conditions) never motivate people. All they do is make people more comfortable (and insecure). And it's the reason you hear people say, "I hate my job, but Sticky Wicket, Inc., has been good to me, and I can't afford to leave."

"But isn't it unrealistic to try to change organizations?"

No more than trying to stop the chance of atomic war.

The odds, of course, are formidable. But our nation's nerve is in question. Not to *try* to stop our lemminglike rush to personal oblivion within large institutions is like a collective admission that freedom is too harsh and difficult a task.

But repealing fifty years of organizational development is a slightly quixotic aim. Clearly, security is central to the employment strategies of millions of America's best-paid people. The practicality of my suggestion is surely brought into question.

No, I'm not advocating some atavistic return to America's romantic individualistic past. Security is a legitimate goal—it's the main reason we all work. My point is that *organizations provide the wrong kind of security. They make people depend on them, when real personal security is being independent* and *involved.*

"What are the signs of an effective manager, a good employer, someone who manages by subjectives?"

An effective employer:

• Has his control problem (every manager *has* this problem) under control.

• Is not easily intimidated by brains, drive, and talent.

• Admits his mistakes and learns from them; managers make the *right* decision in about one out of three decisions.

• Welcomes problems—that's why he is paid more than you or I.

• Thinks long and hard about decisions he makes and is unafraid to make them and to take responsibility for them when they backfire.

• Lavishes praise on the deserving for outstanding work and is unafraid to chastise drones and downtimers.

• Is never reluctant to give up the tiller to people who know what they are doing; one of his jobs is to hire people who know what they are doing.

• Craves results that count, but never ignores the means to these ends, which means constant attention to matters of equity, ethics, and justice.

• Always concerns himself with the details of a job, never falls back and becomes the "Big Picture" type.

• Hires people for their strengths.

• Likes to give his hired hands the needle now and then and knows how to take it himself.

• Regularly turns over his staff, practices job rotation routinely, and never lets a palace guard stand between him and the information he needs.

• Knows how to cut his losses.

• Knows how to fire someone he likes very much.

• Knows how to help those he fires.

• Solves problems face-to-face.

"Are you saying that there is a conflict between managers and leaders?"

You betcha.

Managers have control problems, try to motivate people with bread and circuses, hate face-to-face confrontation, and choose processes over people every time. They manipulate people, situations, and events.

Leaders find people who motivate themselves. Leaders have convictions, hate compromise, and love justice.

If institutions fail, it is because they are unable to respond to challenge. And institutions, like civilizations, go through stages to ultimate decline—in the last act they commit suicide. Leaders are those hired to reform institutions, to reverse decline, to reform, reform more, and reform more again.

Before we can reform the system, we must first reform ourselves. And when we do, the "system" will change.

Self-management is not an easy task, downright painful, and especially on the job, where it's so easy to shift blame from oneself to the organization. Everything begins and ends with people.

Changing the system means changing ourselves. Ready, set, go! The last one home is a dirty reactionary!

It's an endless job, of course. Every institution is at a certain, but never irreversible stage of decay. So constant reform is the only answer; otherwise the Visigoths, the personnel experts, and the motivational specialists are upon us.

If people on the job change, they *force* other people to change, which is how all organizations—corporations, governments, universities, labor unions, nonprofit enterprises—reform and grow and become something tomorrow they were not yesterday. Organizations in reckless decline (no matter how rosy the profit-and-loss statement) are unable to change because their key people won't. A definition of decadence.

Soon, whatever the objectives of the organizations, managers develop vested interests, and the hidden goals of the institution are to serve those who manage it. But the real purposes of the organization are to *"Take Care of Freddie."*

Knowing how to hire (and be hired) and knowing how to fire (and be fired) are flairs I look for in real leaders. A good man or woman, we keep saying, is hard to find. But a great leader these days is rarer still. Every line employee can become a manager; every manager can become a leader; every institution can be reformed. And maybe *you're* just the man or woman this book was finally all about: the new leader!

"God watches out for fools, drunkards, and the United States of America," according to Bismarck. But God needs a lot of help these days.

Do we have the nerve? Is it a question of suicide? And that is the End. When, in truth, every workday is another Beginning.

INDEX